Personality Traits

THE JOURNAL OF ABNORMAL PSYCHOLOGY AND SOCIAL PSYCHOLOGY

VOL. XVI. APRIL, 1921 NUMBER 1

ORIGINAL ARTICLES

EDITORIAL ANNOUNCEMENT

With this Volume (beginning April 1, 1921) The JOURNAL will extend its field to include that of Social Psychology. In conformity with this policy the title of the Journal will be changed to

THE JOURNAL OF ABNORMAL PSYCHOLOGY AND SOCIAL PSYCHOLOGY

The reasons for combining the two fields are set forth in the following statement:

THE FIELD OF SOCIAL PSYCHOLOGY AND ITS RELATION TO ABNORMAL PSYCHOLOGY

At its inception, less than two decades ago, social psychology was variously defined according to different opinions as to its subject matter. The following classes of data were among those stressed in the various definitions: crowd action, the social bases of human nature, the psychological aspects of social formations and movements, and "planes and currents" of thought and action which arise by virtue of the association of human beings. Through the enterprise of the pioneers these formulations, supplemented by many incidental contributions from others, have grown into a science having as its field a unique set of natural phenomena, and a wide range of practical application. A distinct method also is emerging, though progress here is necessarily slow owing to the large scale and the intangibility of much of the data. Interest in the subject is rapidly growing, and there are many courses given in it in colleges throughout the country. It is doubtful whether this stage of interest and importance would have been attained but for the contemporarydevelopment of a sister science, abnormal psychology. Psychopathologists have in recent years delved deeply into the dynamics of human nature. This statement by no means refers to the Freudian School alone. Social psychology, because it is interested more deeply than any other branch (unless it be educational psychology) in the forces underlying human conduct, has been able to profit in a peculiar way by the discoveries of psychopathology. It seems eminently fitting therefore that a journal should be provided as the direct means of expression for workers in social psychology, and that this organ should be affiliated with THE JOURNAL OF ABNORMAL PSYCHOLOGY.

It is appropriate, in view of this enlargement of scope, to attempt an outline of the various interests now properly included under the head of social psychology. The definition of a science is always an arbitrary matter. Quibbling over what should be included or excluded is futile. The intention here is rather to offer suggestions than to set definite limits.

There is first the foundation-study of human traits in so far as they have importance for social life. The individual is our point of departure. His innate and acquired bases of conduct must be examined. Here instinct, learning, and emotion are important according as they adjust or prevent the adjustment of the individual to the social environment. Gregariousness, sympathy, kindliness, rivalry, and other social traits are fundamental. In a broad sense the personality of the individual as one of the radiant points of social action offers a field for practical and theoretical investigation. The technique of personality study and measurement is undergoing a rapid development. Our knowledge of the subject has been immeasureably broadened by contributions from abnormal psychology. The fears and obsessions, the unconscious mental processes, the disassociations, the persistence of infantile traits repressed or expressed, passivity and activity, relation to reality, balance and compensation in the emotional sphere, all make their appearance and play their part in normal human personality and the adjustments between the personality and the social order.

After the canvass of the individual comes the study of the interaction between the individual and the group. On the conscious side this relation takes the form of social consciousness, and acting upon ideal or imaginal social stimuli (such as the feeling of the attitudes of others, codes of conduct, etc.). The old question of whether and in what sense there exists a group mind or a group personality is here involved. The growth of consciousness of self and its dependence on the consciousness of other selves, as well as the foundation of concepts, meanings, and ideals upon social tradition and acceptance, are kindred problems.

Approached from the standpoint of behavior there is offered the whole field of communication: gesture, speech, language, and facial and bodily expression. These functions have been unjustly neglected by psychologists. They are the substructure of the social order; from them develops the entire mechanism of social control, both in the child and in the race. The psychology of the group influence is primarily a matter of social behavior. How do individuals working or acting in a group influence the mental processes of one another? In this important field an experimental method peculiar to social psychology has already attained some recognition. There are experimental results both for the more mechanical and the more intellectual group occupations.

The behavioristic study of the crowd is an interesting division of social psychology. The latent power of instincts and autonomic drives, the mechanisms of imitation (e. g. circular reflex), suggestion, influence of prestige and large numbers, the facilitation, "contagion," or sympathetic induction of emotional response—all really individual phenomena characteristically evoked only by social stimuli—are the leading topics. In this field also abnormal psychology has made important contributions through its studies upon hypnosis, suggestion, automatisms, repressions, and lapse of conscious control.

If we enter the sphere of more permanent social relations, the many adjustments of the human being to his social environment require an understanding of socio-psychological laws. The adjustments of husband and wife as well as those between parents and children bring us into close touch with contributions from the abnormal psychology of the Freudian school. In the social adjustments of deviating personalities abnormal concepts are also of great value. The psychology of ultra-radical movements, of Bolshevism, spiritualistic fanaticism, and the like, is really that of the abnormal personality and its "falling out" with the regime of society. The failure to adjust to the requirements of the social group is the ground for many departures from the normal. In fact it constitutes in many cases of insanity the leading and most comprehensive symptom of modern diagnosis.

We may consider also larger and more permanent groups such as the caste, the professional society, the nation, and the race. To the study of such bodies sociology has heretofore given considerable attention. It is important however to have a psychological statement of nationality and "the national mind." The role of nations in peace and war, and the problems of a society or league of nations call for aid from the psychological student of these large units. Biology and comparative methods are also brought to bear with social psychology in considering the differentiation, development, and improvement of racial stocks. We are led further in this direction to primitive society and the intricate relations of social and abnormal psychology to folk-lore, tradition, myth, and custom.

There is indeed a large body of problems in the treatment of which social psychology has been employed as an adjunct to sociology. The interest of the sociologists in psychological explanations of social movement, imitation, change and progress constitutes one of the lines of descent of our present social psychology. Psychological interest in these subjects is still rife. There are many theories of the nature and origin of society itself which are drawn from a consideration of human nature. Theories of imitation, consciousness of kind, ejective consciousness, social instincts, gregariousness, familial social origins, *l'egoism,* and a number of others illustrate the contributions of psychology to sociological theory. Invention, leadership, control, and progress are forward-pointing interests of socio-psychological science.

There remain for enumeration the various applications of social psychology. The most important of these are the problems of socialization, in a broad sense the fitting of the behavior of the individual to the social order. Socialization involves likewise a reconstruction or reorganization of the social order so that it shall be better fitted to the individual. In the problems of capital and labor, the formation or trade unions and industrial organizations, the claim of the I. W. W., and the various economic and political reconstructions proposed, we find a complex blending of economic and psychological factors. This general problem involving as it does a conflict of group interests, is a most intricate one. More obvious and hopeful examples of socialization are to be found in the Americanization movement, plans for community organization, and the like.

The laws of group influence and crowd action are not without their importance for government. There is no doubt that legislation in representative democratic bodies is strongly affected (and by no means always for the best) by social influence brought to bear in the conditions (deliberations, discussions, etc.) under which it was enacted. Group discussion and its psychology is an important practical theme. Not only government but other social institutions such as the church, the press, the school, and the university have many aims and problems peculiar to the conditions of human association. Formation of opinion, revivals, school spirit, inculcation of ideals, work in the class-rooms,—these are a few examples. There are other less frequently recognized, but important, applications of social psychology to the work of society. Social Ethics, with its program of amelioration, needs the support of social psychology. A knowledge of the laws both of abnormal and of social behavior is a necessary part of the equipment of the social worker. In many of the professions of individuals, such as medicine, law, public speaking, dramatic performance, executive work, and salesmanship, a working acquaintance with the psychology of human contact is an asset of unusual value. In enterprises and movements comprising large numbers of persons such as political and moral campaigns, patriotic rallies, feminism, prohibition, and military service, the social influence is seen at its strongest. Social psychology should afford not only an understanding, but also a means of directing these great streams of combined human energy. Morale, the psychology of "cause," can be made a driving force in social progress.

Finally, the various social maladjustments of delinquency, mental and characterial defect, criminality, and other forms of social inadequacy should interest the student of social behavior. In this field the endeavors of the students of social psychology combine again most intimately with those of the students of abnormal psychology. The efficacy of punishment and reformation requires suggestion and psycho-analytic re-education in combination with the social psychologist's experience with the laws of social influence and control.

In view therefore both of the present need of an organ for social psychology and of the mutually helpful contacts between that science and abnormal psychology, The Journal is pleased to announce the extension of its scope to include the former, and cordially invites those who are interested in the advancement of social psychology to join the ranks of its readers and contributors.

THE EDITORS.

PERSONALITY TRAITS: THEIR CLASSIFICATION AND MEASUREMENT[1]

BY FLOYD H. ALLPORT AND GORDON W. ALLPORT

I

The Nature and Criteria of Personality

THOSE who have been active of late in measuring intelligence have made great progress in the devolpment of measuring scales but very slight progress in the actual definition of intelligence. In dealing with the elusive term "Personality" we may well expect still less satisfactory clarity of definition, no matter what success we have in its measurement. In the measurement of intelligence we have at least the advantage of scales of performance in various mental functions standardized into age or point scale groups. We have, in other words, a means of comparing an individual with his fellows in certain abilities, even though we may not be so bold as to term those abilities intelligence. We may seek, moreover, for a person's mental level in his relative success of adjustment, either to the problems of the school curriculum or to the general problems of life. In this manner a quantitative statement of at least an hypothetical intelligence may be obtained.

The measurement of personality, however, embraces none of these advantages. Individual differences are so great and personal traits so vaguely related to the solution of problems that the notion of an age scale in personality has no significance. Moreover, personalities of divers sorts succeed equally well in the general adaptation to situations of practical life. It may be added that differences of personality are of a qualitative rather than a quantitative sort. These difficulties stand in the way of the development of a personality measurement based on the correlation between tests and familiar objective criteria such as those of intelligence. We must strive toward a descriptive treatment rather than quantitative. Our aim is personality study and description rather than personality testing.

Since, however, description itself demands a definite point of

[1]Adapted from material presented before the National Association of Principals of Schools for Girls, Atlantic City, February 26, 1921.

view, and a definite appraisal of elements, it is necessary to seek some criterion of these elements—some means of stating as objectively as possible the personality as an entity apart from the tool of analysis which we employ. The true criterion of personality is without doubt to be found in the field of social interaction. We are incapable of giving a complete popular description of personality without indicating the manner in which the personality in question stimulates or influences other human beings and the manner in which the behavior of other human beings produces adjustments or responses in the personality in question. In describing this personality we inevitably take the view-point of those "other human beings." Robinson Crusoe, alone on a desert island, undoubtedly displayed a very measureable degree of intelligence in his adaptation to his environment. It was only with the advent of Friday, however, that his personality could be said to stand forth in its full significance. Not only is the language of personality a social one, but the problems arising from the interaction of various personalities are in the truest sense social problems. They include every form of social maladjustment—from the whims of the eccentric to the worst deeds of the criminal. In general it may be said that the aim of personality measurements is the establishing of adjustments between an individual and his fellows which are a benefit to both.

It follows from what has been said of the necessity of a social sphere for the exhibition and description of personality that our objective criterion of what a personality actually is must be the description in quantified terms of that personality by a group of persons with whom he is wont to come into contact. It is with the average of the ratings of such a group of persons that our instruments of analysis must be correlated. Human beings to be sure are subject to prejudice, to quick deduction from scant data, and to great differences in powers of discrimination and judgment. These sources of error must be overcome by improvement in the technique of personality rating; they do not constitute a ground for discarding what must be admitted the only available objective criterion of personality.

Without going into detail as to the removal of these difficulties it may be in place here to note two suggestions of method:

(1) The raters of personality in any given experiment must be fairly numerous, in order to give certainty to the average or median, and to permit the discarding of widely variant ratings.

(2) The raters must have had actual opportunity to observe

the behavior of the subjects, and preferably after having received instructions as to the salient traits which it is desired to rate.

II

The Composition of Personality

Having defined the objective standards of personality to which our methods of measurement must conform, it is necessary now to determine tentatively at least the fundamental traits with which we have to deal. Many of the studies up to the present time have made the error of a superficial and hasty selection of traits. They have been content to rate subjects on such attributes as truthfulness, neatness, conscientiousness, loyalty, perseverance, tactfulness, and the like. It is of course possible to rate individuals with respect to these traits, and for practical purposes such a rating would be valuable. (It will generally be found, however, that attributes of this nature are subordinated on the one hand to particular sets of conditions under which perseverence, truthfulness, loyalty, etc., are manifest, and on the other hand to some of the more pervasive, more deeply lying, and far less evident, tendencies of the personality. Neatness, for example, may be due to such diverse causes as (1) the persistence of the parental ideal, and passive attitude toward parental authority, (2) a phobia toward dirt, arising as a defense reaction against infantile habits, (3) the compensatory striving of a plain-looking girl to make herself attractive in all ways possible, (4) an extreme sensitivity to the social behavior and attitudes of one's fellows. Thus we see that the deeper and more pervasive tendencies are of far greater importance than the superficial attributes which themselves are merely the product of more fundamental tendencies in their play upon the particular environment. The currents of the river are more significant than the eddies and bubbles which arise through the irregularities of the river bed and shore.

Character is the interplay of the fundamental personality tendencies in the social and economic environment, as seen from the point of view of ethics and legal right. Though fundamental from the practical standpoint, it is superficial in that there are deeper currents beneath it. The tragedies of Hamlet, Macbeth, and Othello indicate what divers trends of personality may underlie a single act which from the standpoint of character alone would brand each of the three protagonists as a murderer.

Let us now consider a tentative outline of those fundamental and pervasive tendencies which constitute the main currents of human personality. The following scheme has been used in the Harvard Psychological Laboratory as a working basis.

PERSONALITY

I. Intelligence

II. Temperament
   1. Emotional Breadth
   2. Emotional Strength

III. Self Expression (Strength)
   3. Extro-Introversion
   4. Ascendance—Submission
   5. Expansion—Reclusion.
   6. Compensation
   7. Insight and Self-Evaluation

IV. Sociality
   8. Social Participation
   9. Self-seeking and Aggressive self-seeking
   10. Susceptibility to social stimuli

While it should be emphasized that the traits of the above list lay no claim to final comprehensiveness, they have however the advantages of being fairly exclusive of one another and of standing for fundamental and dynamic forces underlying behavior. We shall proceed to the task of their definition in connection with the possibility of measuring them.

III

Definition and Measurement of the Traits Classified

At the start the investigator is only vaguely aware of the things he intends to measure, and he can only guess at test problems and procedures which will indicate the traits which he selects. The persons who do the rating with which the test results are to be correlated in their turn have but a feeble notion of the characteristics to be sought, and are inexperienced in interpreting human behavior in the light of these characteristics. It is not surprising therefore that at the start correlations should be infrequent and low. A correlation of .30 or .40, although far below the requirement of a more advanced measurement technique, may be taken with a considerable degree of optimism as justifying a further development of the test.

The ratings upon which most of the correlations of the following account were based were obtained in the following manner: Each student of a class of fifty-five men, representing all academic grades, but particularly Sophomores and Juniors, was given three copies of the Personality Rating Scale shown in Appendix A. These scales were given by the student to three associates with the request to rate him as indicated, and in as frank and careful a manner as possible. Envelopes bearing a distinguishing mark were also given out, and the rater in each case was to sign his report, seal it, and return it by the student to the experimenter. These instructions were carefully carried out by nearly all of the students, and their hearty co-operation throughout the tests was secured. It may be said, however, that three ratings for each student is an inadequate number to establish the reliability of tests with much certainty.

For each of the subjects the average of the three estimations of each trait was computed. The names of all the subjects were listed with the averages, one list on a separate sheet for each trait. This procedure facilitated computing the rank and the correlation with the ranking obtained in the test for that trait. It also rendered easier the many trials for ascertaining correlation by inspection with various other data. Owing to the small number of raters, in all cases where there was a discrepancy of twenty-five between any two of the three ratings, the results of the individual concerned were discarded for that trait.

Turning now to the measurement procedure, as might be expected, many more methods of personality testing were devised and tried out than were found in the end successful. The writers lay no claim therefore to any series of personality scales which will adequately cover the classification given above. If they shall be able to demonstrate a few tolerably successful tests with some helpful suggestions for the elaboration of others, they will have accomplished their purpose.

In addition to the procedure described each student was required to write the answers to the questionnaire, selected questions from which are exhibited in Appendix B. It may be remarked that the questionnaire method, though somewhat under suspicion at present, can be made of service in supplementing the evidence from the tests and ratings. It also provides a glimpse of the personality in action, a human touch which adds color and meaning to the quantitative analysis of the various traits. Valuable results, however, can be obtained only if the questionnaire is stated in "behaviortistic" rather than "introspective" terms. To ask the subject whether he is honest, moral, thoughtful, literary in tastes, etc., or to analyze himself by inward searching, is only to encounter the obstacles of carelessness, rationalization, and defense reactions. The questions asked should be in terms of what the subject actually does in his daily life; let the subject judge himself as another person might—by his habitual behavior.

Let us proceed now to a consideration of the traits and tests in detail. The order will follow that of the classification given in Part II.

Intelligence

It was considered important to provide a test of intelligence for purpose of correlation with the various other categories. Professor W. F. Dearborn's Group Test of Intelligence, General Exam., No. 5, was used. This intelligence test, though excellent for immature subjects for whom it was designed, proved to be inadequate as a test of intelligence of our group. The differentiation in the results of individuals had to be obtained by limiting the time, so that the results indicated little difference but that of ability in speed of performance. There was no correlation between the scores thus obtained and the ranking in any of the traits. Intelligence, however, should be considered as one of the most significant factors in personality, since it determines the quality and success of so many of the general adjustments of the individual.

Temperament

1 & 2 *Emotional Breadth and Strength.* The traits numbered one and two in the classification are intended to cover a rather modern treatment of temperament. They occupy the second and third places respectively in the personality rating scale (Appendix A). The rather vague notion of quick and slow in emotion is replaced by the breadth or spread of emotionality. It is thought that the number and variety of objects which to the individual are emotionally toned presents a

valuable dimension in the analysis of his temperament. It will be seen later that there are relations between the emotional tendency and the extroverted and ascendant types.

As to the tests employed there was little that was found to have value. The Pressey Affective Spread Test (see Bibliography) was used, but no significant correlation obtained.

Self Expression (Strength)

Under our third large division of Personality are included a number of rather loosely related traits indicating the subject's most general type of "ego-expression" and adjustment. The essential contrast made in this division is that between the assertive, self-expressive, and generally expansive and dominant type on the one hand, and the withdrawing, secretive, and yielding personality on the other. The former type is one which a new acquaintance readily grasps, and which he finds convincing and forceful. In popular language he is a man "with a personality." With the latter type one is rarely *en rapport,* and the personality seems baffling or else purely negative and weak. It must be understood that these traits are by no means always associated in this manner in individuals we meet, but the distinction presented has a certain rough practical value.

Extroversion—Introversion. The extroverted person is one whose mental images, thoughts, and problems find ready expression in overt behavior. Mental conflicts trouble him but little, and he appears to have nothing to repress or to avoid. The introvert, on the other hand, dwells largely in a realm of imagination, creating inwardly a more desirable ideal world rather than adjusting himself outwardly to the real one. He is not always a misfit, however, for given sufficient ability, his internal or covert reactions may be the vision of the poet or artist. On the whole he takes many things too personally, is anxious and self-searching, if not actually afraid of the repressions and conflicts which have not found a salutory neural outlet or resolution.

This valuable distinction, derived from Freudian psychology and first made clear by the writings of McDougall and Jung, has within recent years opened up a remarkable vista for the understanding of humanity. Owing to its importance many tests were sought by us, and many possible correlations scrutinized, but with little result. A general difficulty lies in the impossibility of knowing whether a certain negative reaction in a test is due to a repression or to an actual absence of that element in the individual concerned. This opposition between Freudian and non-Freudian reactions pervades a great deal of the work in personality study, and renders many apparently ingenious tests almost impossible to interpret. Another reason for the lack of correlation lies in the ratings by associates. This trait is not ordinarily recognized by any but trained raters who have an intimate knowledge of the subject. It is not so much the absence of overt behavior that marks the introvert as the presence of rich and persistent internal responses; and the latter of course is the most difficult to detect, being accessible only to one who is subtle enough to read the subject from small and unconscious clues.

4. *Ascendance-Submission.* When a person comes into a face to face relation with another person whom we may suppose is his equal in every way there is generally a real, though sometimes scarcely conscious, conflict between the two egos. This is true both because each is endowed with the fundamental drives of humanity which are essentially self-seeking, and also because two persons are rarely sufficiently alike to establish a perfect harmony of responses. Social behavior is not a process like the movements of cog-wheels in machinery, but a conflict and adjustment of variant attitudes of individuals. In conflicts, generally speaking, there emerge a victor and a vanquished; and this is true of the face to face dual reactions described. One of the two opponents becomes the master; his interest dominates, and he carries his point. The other yields and accordingly is dominated, though by no means always against his will. The former personality we describe as ascendant. In terms of social behavior he is *active*. The latter is said to be submissive; his attitude in the face to face relation is *passive*. (This trait is No. 1 in the Personality Rating Scale.)

It must be understood that a person may be ascendant in some situations and submissive in others. The most dominant man among his peers may be thrown into the passive attitude even by the recollection of his parents or early teachers. We may safely say, however, that in dealing with equals, and in the aggregate of their responses, most men may be said to fall in one or the other of these two classes. The principle is well illustrated among children by dynamometric strength contests. In contests of two boys facing each other, each with an instrument in his hand, it is found that, almost at the beginning of the trial, one boy feels overcome by the masterful strength of the other, and adopts the attitude of making a respectable score rather than of standing at the top. In every walk of life the "leading" type and the "following" type may be readily noted.

Test of Ascendance-Submission. For the purpose of measuring this trait an Active-Passive Reaction Study was devised. This study consisted of the description of a number of typical situations in each of which the ascendant-submissive relation was involved. The subject was asked to react in a spontaneous, emotional manner to these situations, and to write down immediately the way in which he would conduct himself if faced with the conditions described. This type of test, to be sure, presupposes the co-operation of the subjects, and an interest on the part of each in actually analyzing and truthfully presenting his own type of behavior rather than in merely making a good impression.

Following are two of the typical situations presented in the Active-Passive Study. They will serve to give the reader a general idea of the test method as well as of the nature of the ascendant-submissive relation which we are now considering.

(2) Suppose you are 10 years of age now, but with the traits you actually had at that age. You are playing war with some boys the same age. (a) Are they likely to make you fight on the side of Germany? (b) If they do, what will you do about it?

(3) Upon leaving college you become a salesman and are trying to sell a life insurance policy to a middle-aged financier of great note. He says, "Young man, I don't know how long you have been in the game, but you will never succeed unless you acquire more experience and confidence in yourself." What will you say or do?

In the first situation (fighting on the side of Germany) an interesting series of scores was derived. It was found that the individuals who appeared on the basis of their answers in the Reaction Study as a whole to fall in the ascendant group reacted usually by recording an active struggle to keep from being made a German, or at least a refusal to play the game under such humiliating circumstances. The submissive individuals were, in three cases out of every four, those who simply acquiesced and played the role of the German. Another response indicating the trait of submission, though to a less degree, was the attitude of acceptance with the idea of making Germany win.

The second situation proved likewise to be suggestive. The answer indicating an undisturbed persistence in trying to sell the insurance scored + 12 (i. e. appeared twelve times as often in the replies of the ascendant individuals as in the replies of the submissive); taking the defensive scored + 6; acknowledging the criticism with thanks scored —4 (i. e. appeared four times as often in the replies of the submissive individuals as in the replies of the ascendant); apologetic attitude, —6; emotional reaction, angry leave-taking, etc. scored —10.

It is significant that when all the situations had been scored there was usually a sufficient incidence of the ascendant and submissive answers in the case of any individual subject to allow for a fairly consistent and certain decision as to the type to which the individual belonged. When the subjects were all ranked from the most ascendant to the most submissive on the basis of these scores the correlation with the ranking by Personality Rating was found to be .40. Considering the tentative nature, both of the situations used and the method of scoring, as well as the inadequacy of the technique of rating, this correlation is high enough to justify further development of tests of this nature.

5. *Expansion-Reclusion.* This trait is easily recognized, but requires careful definition. As stated in the Personality Rating Scale (trait 8) the expansive person is one whose "ego" or whose "personal touch" enters into all that he says or does. The successful minister or politician, as well as the executive and artist in the general sense, belong to this type. When, however, the person is not gifted, and is by chance aggressive as well as expansive, he is socially objectionable. The reclusive person either consciously or otherwise keeps himself in the background. He fulfills his office in a perfunctory manner without extending himself into his work. He is by no means, however, necessarily secretive or introverted, or even submissive. The expansive person usually writes a questionnaire or other personal documents in a manner charged with personal feeling, thought, and even reference. There is a certain richness in this sort of reaction; we feel a fullness of contact with the person. He may be said to have a definite or outstanding personality. The writings of the reclusive individual, however adequate objectively, are poor in self-feeling and expression. His manner as well as his style leave us unsatisfied or in doubt; we have not made a satisfactory contact with the person. Probably this trait, expansion-reclusion, more than any other is the key-note in the judgment of personality by one's fellows.

Test of Expansion-Reclusion: We endeavored to get a measurement of this quality by asking the subjects each to write a letter answering an advertisement of a position, a letter in which one would be free to tell as much or as little about one's self as desired. The advertisement which was answered was worded as follows:

Wanted: Young men for detective work; good government positions ahead. No experience required. Address, Ganor, St. Louis, Box 777.

The instruction was to answer this advertisement as seriously and with as natural a reaction as if actually seeking the position. The subject could say as much or as little as he chose.

The letters produced were read and scored by a group of twelve graduate students in psychology on the basis of the trait of expansion-reclusion. The score of 1 was given to a letter indicating the most expansive personality which they could imagine to occur in a group of 50; the score of 50 indicating the most reclusive. The following expressions of this trait were borne in mind in rating the letters: a considerable number of references to self, statement in detail of qualifications, particularly those of a rather personal sort, and the development of subjective ideas, feelings, and interests in relation to detective work. The absence of these characteristics combined with general meagerness or brevity, and the general impression of conveying little about the personality, were grounds for scoring the letter on the reclusive side of the scale.

Examples of the expansive and reclusive types of letter are given below:

Letter of D (Expansive)

Mr. Ganor, Box 777,
St. Louis,
Dear Sir:—

In replying to your ad, I should like to say that I am desirous of undertaking this work because I feel introspectively capable of doing the work. I think that this line of occupation is one that cannot fail to keep up my interest—is one extremely variegated and opening up new channels of adventure at each succeeding step—of which, I must say, I am extremely fond. I do not hesitate to say that I am positively certain of being able to do the work knowing as I do that I am gifted for it and shall undertake it, if successful in obtaining the position, in the full confidence that I *will* make good. I must acknowledge, however, that I have had no practical experience whatever in this line, but I think my lack in this respect will be compensated for by my enthusiasm for undertaking this work. Hoping to hear favorably from you.

Very sincerely yours,

Letter of R (Reclusive) (See Personality Graph IV of same subject).

Mr. Ganor,
Box 777,
St. Louis, Mo.
Dear Sir:—

Having seen your advertisement for men for detective work, I am writing you that you may consider me as one of the men desirous of entering that work. At present I am a senior at Harvard University expecting to finish my course about the st of June. Until that time I would not be able to consider entering your service, at if you do not expect to enroll men immediately, I would be glad if you would keep ie in mind, knowing that you could count on me surely by the end of June, 1921.

Sincerely,

The correlation between the average ratings of the letters made by the twelve judges and the Personality Rating was .34, which again must be considered suggestive in the light of the crude and tentative methods.

In connection with this important trait a few suggestions may be added. In certain cases we have known the handwriting of expansive persons to be unusually large and, to use Dr. June E. Downey's expression, uninhibited or impulsive. In regard to motor expression in general, certain expansive persons when tested have shown pronounced tendencies to over-estimation in kinaesthetic reproduction of distances; certain cautious persons are prone to underestimate. The exact relation between these kinaesthetic judgments and the personality trait we are now considering needs to be worked out in greater detail before we can generalize. Another indicator of expansive egotism is found in the number of "I's" used, or other direct references to self, in reports given by the various students in regular seminary courses. The number of ego-references were obtained only when the reports of the individuals were on equally objective topic and were considered per unit of time. A count of this kind, the victims of course being unaware, was made. Certain individuals make with surprising constancy as high as eighty or ninety ego-references per one-half hour of speaking; others make as low as four or five; the median approximates the lower end of the scale, being about ten.

6. *Compensation*: The trait of compensation is not mentioned in the Personality Rating Scale, nor have we any satisfactory tests to offer. Its presence is indicated in thoroughly answered questionnaires, but owing to the fact that it can be understood only through a knowledge of the complete history of the individual, it is extremely difficult to bring to a focus in any measurement procedure. The method of discovering whether compensations are present must take into account two factors: first, the limitation or defect, physical, mental, social, or financial, which was or still is, present in the case before us, and secondly, the nature and perseverence of the process of overcoming the difficulty, or satisfying the fundamental demands of the ego through vicarious channels. A complete discussion of this trait would take us too far afield. It is not clear whether there is such a

thing as a generally compensating personality or whether the com-pensation is dependent only upon the peculiar circumstances, defects and abilities, of a given case. The self-made man is probably one of the best examples, and suggests a general compensatory attitude. Few of the deep-lying currents of the individual's life are of such importance as this. It is the chief basis of what is popularly known as "character building."

The following case illustrates this process. It was only after a careful study that the compensatory mechanism was discovered. For such practical issues as the one here involved, and for understanding people generally, a test of this trait would be most desirable.

G. L. came to the office greatly agitated over the fact that his mark in psychology course was reported as a D+. He said that he must have a C— in order to be retained on the list of the Federal Board, the government's agency for furnishing an education to young men who had fought in the war and had incurred some wound or other considerable sacrifice. On one previous occasion G. L. had drawn attention to himself. The class was given some group intelligence tests, and he had tried the first problem only, for finding that he was very slow, he had refused to finish the tests, writing at the top a lengthy but rather stupid excuse, saying that he was in no condition, the test would not be fair, etc.

In general appearance G. L. was slow-moving, stodgy, and rather oppressed looking. His complexion was pale, and had the unwholesome inelasticity of putty. His reactions, both mental and physical, were very slow. He was considerably above the age of the average college student. The general impression he created was certainly not favorable; every aspect of his personality was against him. An investigation of his case revealed the following facts:

Born of humble parentage, of low caste socially, with an inferior physique, and exceedingly slow in mental reactions—though not distinctly defective, this young man had struggled for years to maintain employment. His efforts were persistent and conscientious, but without avail. Though faithful and patient G. L. was repeatedly laid off when he failed to keep up with a rush in business. His chief drawbacks in the business world (as stated objectively by himself) were (1) slowness and (2) "lack of personality."

During the war, after serving *near* the front for two or three months, a shell burst a little distance away from him, and he developed a nervous break down, a typical case of shell-shock with some paralysis. After recovery he was discharged, but entered government employ again as a crude laborer in a munitions factory. One day, his story goes, he was carrying a large shell when it slipped and dropped on *both* his feet injuring him painfully. After being again discharged, G. L. worked for months to be placed upon the Federal Board and so incur the advantages of the disabled soldier. These advantages G. L. told off earnestly and significantly on his fingers: the government would agree to give the wounded ex-service man a college and technical education, aggregating if necessary 5 years, paying all expenses, tuition, books and living; and if the man made good the government would keep him in some form of employment with good remuneration the rest of his life. Furthermore, and *most significant,* in all civil service examinations ex-service men of his class would have a 10 per cent. lower passing grade than other men. (Just the handicap which G. L. figured that he needed to secure a position in competition with brighter men!

The occupation which he himself suggested—and which in this round about way he was laboring to attain—was an assistantship of some sort keeping records of some government museum. This certainly would be an ideal sinecure for an educated inferior mind of great slowness.

The mechanism here is fairly obvious. There was in G. L.'s case recognized inferiority of personality, social caste, physique, and mental reactions, for which he compensated by a remarkable program of events, most if not all of which rested more fully in his own hands than he himself would admit. We may perhaps hazard the assumption that the Freudian mechanism of wish-fulfillment underlay his shell-shock experience as well as the accident wherein the disability was incurred which placed him permanently under the protection of the Federal Board.

This shrewdness in so shaping events as to compensate for inherent defects may perhaps not win our full approval. And yet is it not remarkable how effectively the compensatory tendency has operated so as to enable the man by cunning and perseverance to provide a position for himself where he might become a respectable citizen in the career of government employ, rather than the casual laborer, mendicant, or even criminal, to which his defects would otherwise condemn him? In place of the cowardly inertia which appeared at first sight, we find all the dynamic energy of the evolutionary struggle for existence condensed into one human personality. To the Socratic dictum "Know Thyself" he has added "and Compensate Therefor."

7. *Insight and Self-Evaluation.* The term insight indicates the degree to which a person is able correctly to appraise his traits of personality. (See Trait No. 5 in Personality Rating Scale.) It is derived from the use in psychopathology in which it signifies the extent to which a person realizes that his delusion or hallucination is or has been a fiction of the imagination. A person with good insight is not likely to be deceived by his own rationalization and by the self-extenuation of his acts by refusing to recognize their motives. The possession of this trait or the modification of the personality so as to acquire it has deep practical significance. The process of reformation of a criminal or of character improvement in the socialized individual, is possible only when one's personality is revealed to one's own eyes. The measurement of this trait was provided for as follows: Each of the subjects made out for himself a personality rating scale. In his ratings he differs more or less from the average of the estimations of the three raters in the various traits. The average of his deviations for the various traits gives a practical index of his insight, the lower the average the higher the insight.

Closely related to Insight is the trait of Self-Evaluation, indicated in the Rating Scale as No. 9. The individual here is asked to rate his *abilities*, for example, his general intelligence, rather than his traits of personality. This estimation, of course, must be made prior to the giving of the intelligence test. The self-evaluation index of each individual is expressed by the difference between his actual rank in the group in intelligence test score and his self-ranking, prefixing a + or — according to whether he over or under-rated himself.

There are some pertinent conclusions from work done in the Harvard Laboratory in previous similar investigations. An interesting relation exists between the degree of intelligence and the self-evaluation index. There is a striking tendency for those who are high in intelligence to have a negative index, that is, to underestimate themselves, and for those who are low in intelligence, to have a high index. This finding is in harmony with the result of Hollingworth in his self-evaluation in various desirable traits. The possession of the trait in question seemed to insure a more accurate recognition of it, both in self and others; while those low in the desired qualities tended to overrate themselves. The actual inverse correlation between intelligence and self evaluation index which we obtained from an earlier experiment upon thirty subjects was —.67.

The following chart, Fig. 1, shows this inverse relation of intelligence to self-evaluation. The dotted line indicates the relative intelligence of a group of sixteen subjects (according to the Otis Group Tests), and the blocks their corresponding self-evaluation indices. The horizontal line represents both the median of the Otis scores and the point above which the self-evaluation index is positive, i. e. indicates over self-evaluation, and below which this index shows negative or under self-evaluation.

Sociality

The final group of traits is intended to call attention to the individual in his rôle as a unit of society. The self-expressive group dealt with the general types and levels of adjustments of the individual to his world. Sociality, however, is intended to bring out the specific reactions which show how much an individual is dominated in his behavior by considerations purely of self and by aggressive self-interest which overrides the interests of others and seems to be incapable of modification by social stimulation and control. The other side of the picture of course is an actual interest in the welfare of others and an inclination to be stimulated by their presence and behavior. In this group lie the foundations of the ethical aspect of character, high ideals, principles, and the like.

8. *Social Participation.* In this practical field actions must speak louder than words. A most important indication of sociality is amount of time and energy (not money or good wishes) which the

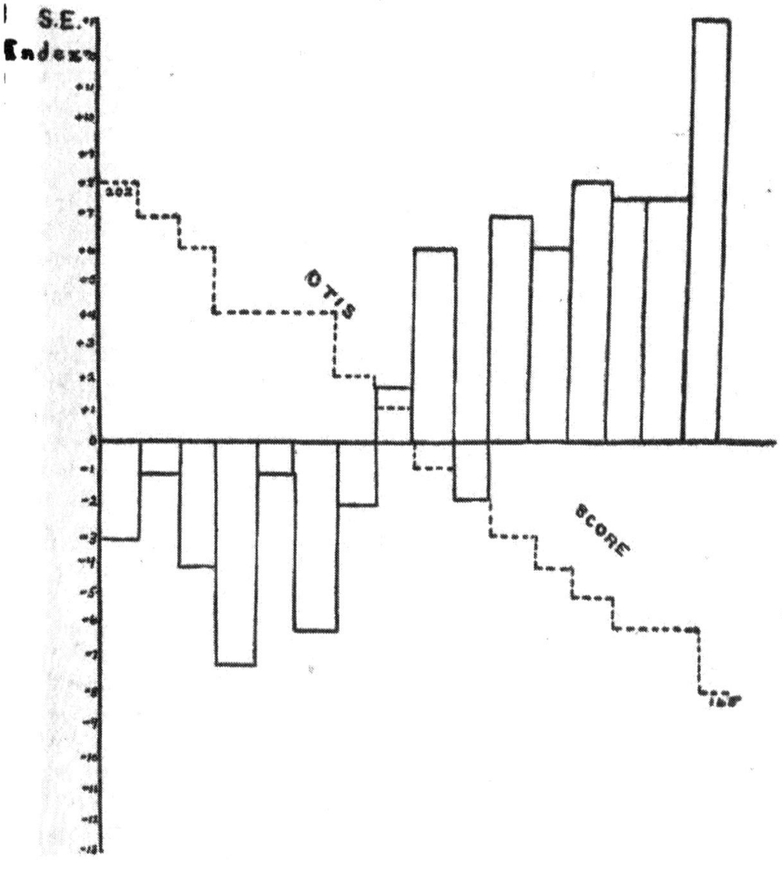

Figure 1. Showing the Relation between Intelligence and Self-evaluation in 16 subjects.

(For an explanation see text).

individual gives to social activities. By "social activities" is me not merely attendance at dances, clubs, and the like, where the beh ior of others is a matter of secondary interest only; but more espec ly actual occupation with the guidance, understanding, control, a amelioration of other human beings. It is an interest in the soc behavior and welfare as such. Participation is the trait sought, n mere passive interest. It is indicated as trait No. 6 on the Personal Rating Scale.

An analysis of the questionnaire reports indicated that 56 p cent. more individuals in the group expressed an interest in soci activities than actually took active part in them. Naturally enoug there appears to be no reliable test of this trait other than observin the habits of the person or accepting his statement therefor. A corr lation was found between the Personality Rating for extroversion an that for social participation amounting to .40. In comparing th results of the questionnaire (questions 15 and 17) with the graphs o personality, to be described later, the following relations were found

Of the nine reporting participation in social work,

6 were ascendant; 3 were submissive (2 of these expansive).
7 were of strong type; 2 were of weak type.

By "strong" and "weak" type are meant individuals who were respec tively high and low in the group of traits under self-expression take as a whole.

9. *Self-seeking and Aggressive Self-seeking.* Selfishness with out being distinguished from aggressive selfishness is the tenth trait or the Personality Rating Scale. A test of this trait is much to be de sired. Upon it depends very largely the success or failure of a perso as a citizen of the community. When the self-seeking person is in capable of forming habits modifying his natural egoistic tendencie to accord with social influences, and when as a result he pursues thes tendencies in opposition to the socially recognized rights of others, he becomes a criminal. It seems quite possible that a tactful adaptatio of the principle used in the Active-Passive Reaction Study might afford a useful measurement.

10. *Susceptibility to Social Stimuli.* A great deal might be written about the degree to which a personality is habitually sensitiv to the behavior, suggestions, gestures, emotional expression, and phys iognomy of others. Obviously one can neither understand men nor control his own actions in accord with the social regime unless he ca

be stimulated to respond to these objects. Inasmuch as such stimulability is a prerequisite for the successful adjustment of an individual to his social environment it may be termed a kind of "social intelligence." Our efforts toward the measurement of this ability have consisted of a test of judging facial expressions. The material and possibilities of such a test, as well as the nature of the process of facial interpretation, are discussed in two articles by Professor H. S. Langfeld (see Bibliography). We have followed his suggestion and devised a test, not however in the nature of naming the facial expressions, as this involves linguistic ability, but by underlining the name of the expression most fitting the picture out of a list of eight possible expressions. Fourteen pictures, photographed from sketches of a German actor representing various moods and emotions were chosen as material.

The only correlation which we could detect in this test was that between ability in judging facial expressions and artistic ability, particularly of the literary type. Of the nine men who made the highest scores in the facial expressions test, seven had literary ability to the extent of actually having produced and gained some recognition by publication or otherwise. There was only one case of a low score in facial expressions where the individual had also a record of literary production.

IV

The Graphical Representation of Personality

Aside from the main purpose of developing tests or measurements of personality one of the most valuable possibilities in a study of this sort is representing in graphical terms the degrees of the various traits which go to make up that unique thing—a human personality. Personalities, like faces, have no duplicates; each one is a unique mixture of varying degrees of divers traits. It is at least conceivable, however, that there may be a general agreement of individuals in the rough pattern produced by graphing their qualities. We may perhaps expect certain traits to follow the same general level as others. Where this is true we may be said to have discovered types. Our chief aims, therefore, in graphical representation shall be: first, a picture of the individual personality and its checking up by the questionnaire or other information; second, the discovery of striking or unusual personalities and strongly contrasting personalities; and third,

to find out what general types if any the various combinations of tra
may reveal.

Inasmuch as the tests themselves are in too primitive a state
development to justify their graphical representation, the ratings
the various traits plotted on the following charts were based on th
average of the three personality ratings of a given individual. Th
first point in the graph, corresponding to Intelligence, however, wa
taken from the actual intelligence tests. As suggested above, owin
to the fact that the test was not adapted to his particular group, thi
point on the graph must not be taken too seriously. Both the poin
corresponding to the degree of insight and the point denoting self-
evaluation are Personality Ratings on these points and not the indice
described above.

The trait of compensation was not rated and hence is not shown in the graphs. Aggressive self-seeking was not differentiated in the ratings or graphs from simple self-seeking. There was a general tendency to rate the individuals too high in this trait, that is, as too unselfish. The true median therefore lies somewhat above that shown on the charts. Susceptibility to social stimuli is indicated by the actual rank in the class in the score of the facial expressions test.

Explanation of the Personality Graphs. The four main groups of traits, namely Intelligence, Temperament, Self-expression, and Sociality are indicated as sections in the order stated from left to right, separated by heavy vertical lines. It will be convenient often to regard these sections as wholes. The facial expression test column is separated from the other members of the sociality group by a heavy line, because it seemed better in this case to leave it out of account in considering social and non-social types.

The manner in which the graphs were plotted is as follows: In the vertical columns are given the various traits,—at the top, one extreme (that coinciding with a rating of 1 in the Personality Rating Scale), and at the bottom the opposite extreme (50 in the Rating Scale). The horizontal line through the middle indicates the median rating (25) in the trait concerned. To take an example in the first graph, subject F was among the lowest five in the group in the intelligence test score, was rated two or three above the median in the strength of emotions, about 10th from the top in extroversion, and in self evaluation about 30th from the top (i. e. from the most over self-evaluated).

Following is given a key to the abbreviations used in the vertical columns of the charts:

H. Int.	=	high score in Intelligence Test
L. Int.	=	low score in Intelligence Test
B. Emot.	=	Broad Emotions (emotional breadth)
N. Emot.	=	Narrow Emotions (lack of emotional breadth)
S. Emot.	=	Strong Emotions
W. Emot.	=	Weak Emotions
Asc.	=	Ascendant
Sub.	=	Submissive
Ext.	=	Extroverted
Int.	=	Introverted
Exp.	=	Expansive
Rec.	=	Reclusive
G. Ins.	=	Good in Insight
P. Ins.	=	Poor in Insight
+ S. E.	=	Over Self-evaluation
— S. E.	=	Under Self-evaluation
Soc. Part.	=	Social Participation
Non. Soc. Part.	=	Lack of social participation
Non. Self-seek.	=	Lack of Self-seeking
Self-seek.	=	Self-seeking
G. Fac. Exp.	=	Good at judging facial expressions
P. Fac. Exp.	=	Poor at judging facial expressions

The seven graphs reproduced below were selected from those of fifty-five subjects and serve to illustrate some of the individual characteristics. When the graphs were sorted two main types were apparent. It was found that the traits under Self-expression went fairly uniformly together. There were of course exceptions. On the whole, however, we can distinguish the strong type (e. g. F and S.) and t weak type (e. g. H. and R.), with the self-expression traits as a who respectively above and below the median. In the following expla tions these two types are designated as extroverted and introverte this trait being regarded as most salient. A further classification c be made in which are to be found distinct types, i. e. the social a a-social. The former consists of those having social participatio and non-self-seeking above the median, the latter of those having the traits below the median. Four fairly distinct groups (with a fe transitional cases) may thus be defined as follows:

Strong
1. Extroverted—Social
2. Extroverted—A-social

Weak
1. Introverted—Social
2. Introverted—A-Social

Other special relations of traits are indicated below.

V

Inter-Relations of the Main Divisions of the Personality

A few remarks may be made upon certain relations which were found to exist among the various large divisions of the personality traits. In order to discover whether a given type of temperament went with a self-expression (or strength) type, the graphs were sorted into piles on the basis of both the breadth and strength of emotions. The number of cases showing the different sides (extroverted-introverted, etc.) of the self-expressive traits selected, was counted in each pile. In this way any distinct predominances, for example, of the narrow over the broad emotionality in introversion, was shown. Table I indicates these numerical relations; and the general description of the emotional traits predominantly accompanying the various traits of self-expression is given at the right. The figures indicate the number of individuals having their emotions characterized by the letter at the top of the vertical columns who belong, also to the strength type indicated at the left of the line in which the given figure occurs.

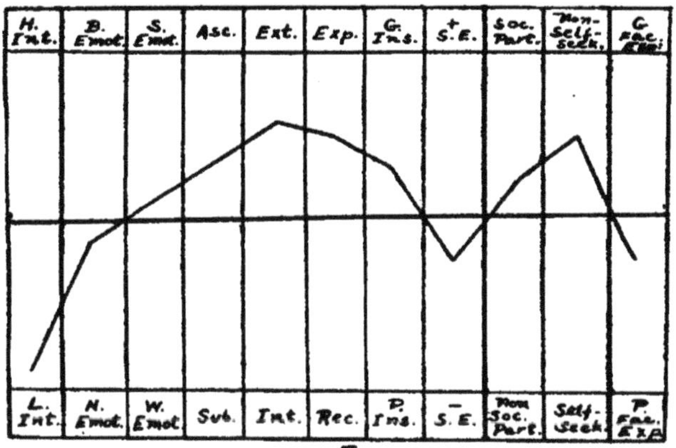

F

GRAPH I.

Subject F belongs to the *extroverted social type*. The narrow breadth of the emotions accompanied by strength is, as will be later shown, characteristic of the strongly extroverted type. The extroverted social type is more numerous than the extroverted a-social.

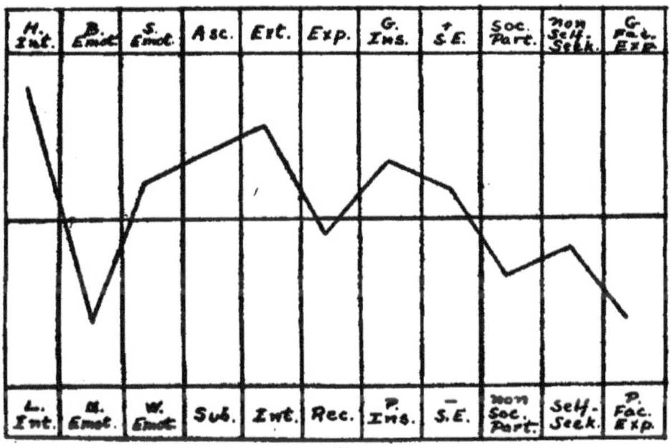

Fo

GRAPH II.

Subject Fo illustrates the *extroverted a-social type*. His personality does not seem to be as strong as that of F owing to the slight reclusion.

Note again the rise of the curve in emotionality, from N. to S. Emotions.

Questionnaire says he is "easily embarrassed." This fact as well as the low sociability seem to accord with reclusive (but not introverted) habits.

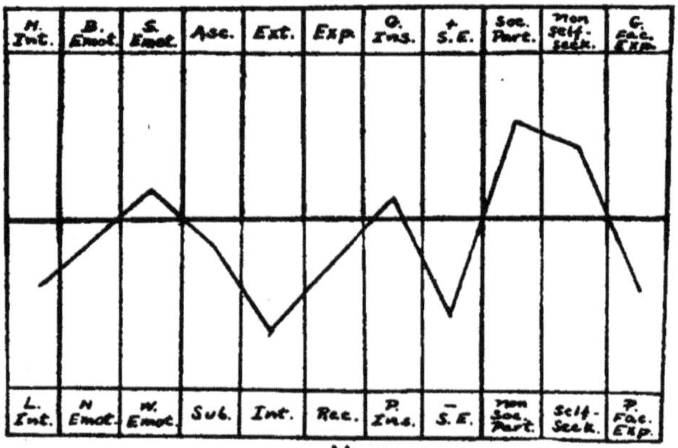

H

GRAPH III.

Subject H. belongs to the rather exceptional *introverted social type*. He is somewhat abnormal, almost a psychopathic personality. Neurotic heredity.

This subject, possessing some insight, is very depressed as well as introverted. His low S. E. index would indicate this. He is totally pessimistic, saying in his questionnaire that he would commit suicide if it were not for his parents. Life holds no interest or attraction for him.

The social interests are to be explained probably as persistences of strong social welfare leanings, political interests, and boys' club activities around the age of ten and in high school. Since entering college he has lost interest in the world about him, become depressed and apathetic. This marked introversion probably was connected with adolescence.

H's questionnnaire reveals some very enlightening facts. First of all, he asked his physician if he ought to write the answers, because having just recovered from a nervous collapse he thought it would be unwise to dwell on his personal troubles too much. He is bashful in the presence of his elders and with girls. It is difficult for him to recover his composure. He feels a nervous tingling and a burning of the cheeks for two or three hours when angry, and does not trust himself to say or do anything for a time. Emotions easily upset. Has day dreams of physical prowess (is actually a frail, weak youth) in which he is fighting a crowd, kicking a goal with a football from any angle within the fifty yard line, shooting goals in basket ball with his back to the basket. States himself these fantasies may be a compensation for poor physique. Has many "fussy" mannerisms, such as biting or tearing nails, biting lips, tearing papers, etc. The sex relation "shocks his sensitivity—unpleasant mental images, etc." He is entirely apathetic toward girls. Has only one girl friend who is five years older than himself. His roommate has had a very detailed book on sex on his desk for several weeks, but H. says he never troubled to open the cover. In his sex reactions H. is decidedly a-typical.

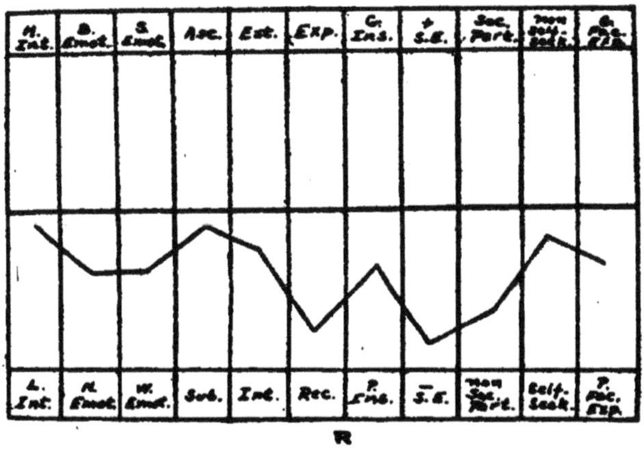

GRAPH IV.

Subject R. is an example of the *introverted a-social type.* This is a very remarkable personality, the only one in the group below the median in all traits. We may suppose it is very difficult to establish any "contact" with this man. The extreme lowness in both reclusion and under self-evaluation are worthy of note. His answers to the questionnaire are very short and laconic. Socially considered, this is a very poor personality.

The low emotionality may of course be due to repression of outward evidence of emotion.

The repression and "touchiness" of the introvert are shown in this man by the fact that he was the only subject in the group of fifty-five who considered any of the questions "too personal" to answer. He placed cross marks (x), the designated sign, in place of answers to questions touching his reactions when angry, and events in his sex life.

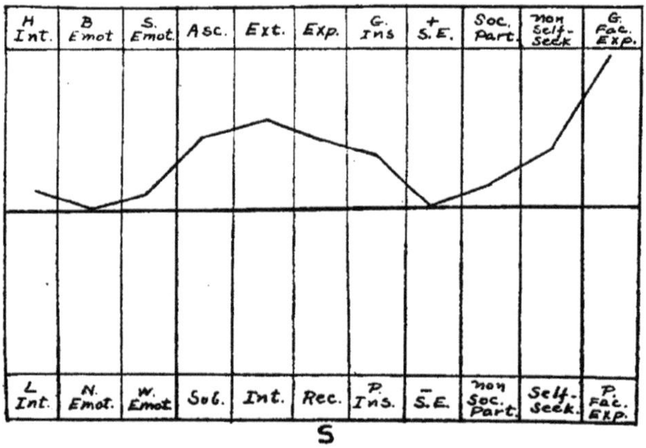

GRAPH V.

Subject S. stands out in marked contrast to subject R. Here is evidently a strong, dominant personality. His questionnaire was particularly expansive, and charged with self feeling and reference, though of an extroverted sort.

In S. we find a combination of literary achievement and an ability to read facial expressions. His perfect self evaluation is worthy of remark.

In his interests he is active, loving prize fights, games of strength, etc. He writes his disagreement with the author in margins of books.

Probably the clue to this titanic individual is found in compensation. Evidently thrown early upon his own resources he has had all kinds of jobs, some very menial, in which he asserts that he has learned human nature. He has probably done more than this in building up a strong personality.

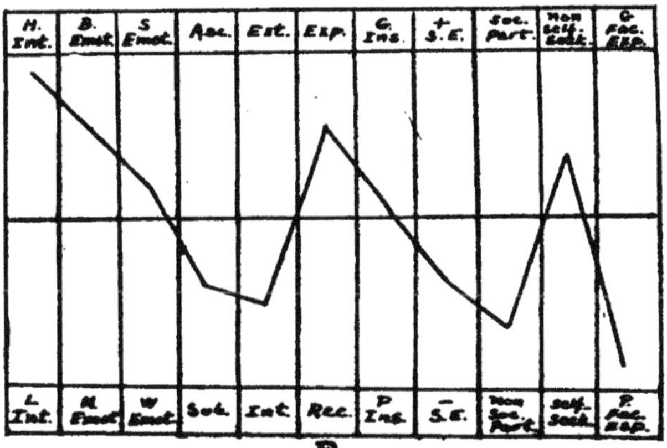

P

GRAPH VI.

Subject P. appears from his graph to be a somewhat stormy and troubled soul. And this is the case. His outstanding emotionality and expansiveness, coupled with his moody introversion and self-depreciation give his personality a uniqueness whether for weakness or for strength.

His type is particularly of interest in showing the combination of deep introversion with wide expansion. We all know a few people of this sort who expand and spread their introverted knot of personality out over the social world. Students of this type often show expansion by asking questions in class which owing to their introverted bearing seem to others unintelligible or even absurd. On the other hand a touch of genius might produce from such a combination a Byron or a Tchaikowsky. P.'s questionnaire, ten pages in length, expands in an introverted outcry against the tedium of college life, and the worthlessness of academic studies leading only to "a piece of sheepskin" with his "name on it in Latin." He wants to get away, get married, to go west, and make money. His introversion is best shown in what he says he would do in imagination in a case of balked anger. His imaginary maltreating of his enemy (which he says he would repress in actual life) is indeed fearful to read. When falsely accused of a misdemeanor he tempered his sullen resentment with a mild glory in his martyrdom.

The discrepancy between the intelligence test and facial expression test scores is interesting.

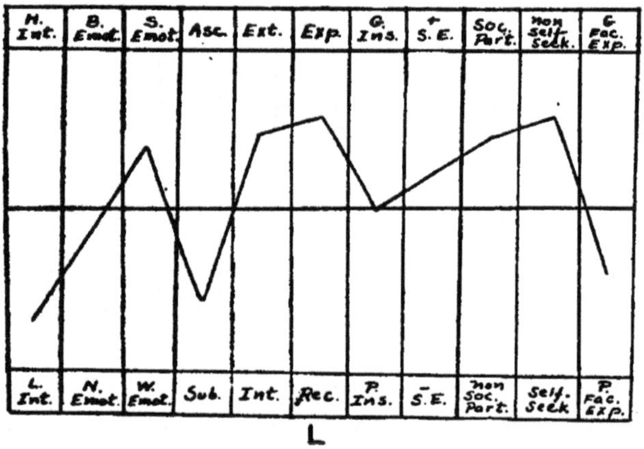

GRAPH VII.

Subject L. shows the combination, also not infrequent, of submission and extroversion. Of the opposite type, ascendant-introverted, we have not found a single clear example.

This individual probably presents a ready social contact, having a combination of traits which should render him easy-going and well liked. He is not troubled by exaggerated emotions; he yields readily, following rather than wishing to lead; he is devoid of the baffling and disturbing repressions of the introvert; he expands his ego forming ready points of contact; and he is socially inclined and unselfish.

STRENGTH-TYPE AND EMOTIONALITY

S. Type	N.	B.*	W.	S.*	Emotionality Traits
Ext.	23	5	14	14	Narrow—Medium Strength (+) see note*
Int.	14	12	16	10	Medium breadth—weak
Asc.	13	9	9	13	Medium breadth—strong
Sub.	14	5	14	5	Narrow—Weak
Med.	9	3	7	5	
Exp.	16	14	16	14	Medium breadth—Med. Strength
Rec.	19	4	14	9	Narrow—Weak
Total	36	17	30	23	

*Owing to the fact that there were in the total many more cases of narrow emotions than broad, and of weak than strong, the figures in these columns are to be given somewhat weighted emphasis.

	Social (33)	A-Social (24)
Strong Type (33)	21	12
Weak Type (24)	12	12

TABLE I

Key:
N = Narrow
B = Broad
W = Weak
S = Strong
Med = Medium

The tendencies expressed in Table I are somewhat more clearly shown in Figure 2, the two extremes of the two emotional traits respectively, being indicated by the letters in blocks. The crossing of the emotional traits in the extrovert and introvert is perhaps the most significant point. Submissive and reclusive differ from introverted in having a narrower range of emotional response.

FIGURE 2

RELATION BETWEEN SELF-ASSERTION AND EMOTIONALITY

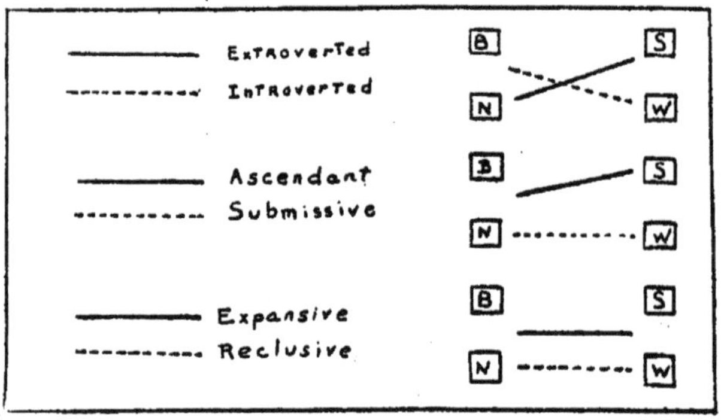

Figure 2. Emotion and Strength-Type.

VI

Suggestions on Personality from the Questionnaire

The answers to certain items of the questionnaire were compared with the personality ratings and with other questionnaire items so as to discover any possible further indications of the inter-relation of personality traits.

Compensations were indicated, mostly arising from childhood tendencies, in about eight or nine cases. They were generally of the athletic sort, and were closely associated with persistent childhood influences (Q. 1), and with creative ability (Q. 5).

Those who reported the foster child fantasy (Q. 25) strangely enough seemed to be of the extroverted type. They were also somewhat ascendant though often reclusive.

There were about eight cases of a-typical sex response and interest (i. e. eight cases recognized as a-typical from their reports). They consisted of those to whom there was something repulsive about the sex relation and those showing unusual indifference or repression in sex events. Of these eight a-typical sex reaction types:

7 were also day-dreamers (strongly persistent)
6 showed introverted responses in anger
6 showed introverted responses in anger and unjust punishment

6 had unstable emotions
4 showed compensatory tendencies.

The following list showing the frequency of occurrence of various types of answers to the questionnaire may prove of interest. Doubtless many of the figures should be higher because of the failure of the subject to remember or truly to analyze himself. The figures indicate that per cent. of the total number of subjects whose answers clearly indicated the presence of the trait or conditioned named.

Item	Questionnaire Number	Percent of occurrences
1. "Interested" in social work	17 (a)	76%
2. Persistent childhood influences and interests	1, 2	53%
3. Day Dreaming (rather strongly persistent)	12	51%
4. Unstable emotions, bashfulness, embarrassment	11, 21, 22	45%
5. Creativeness	5	32%
6. Annotating books	24	28%
7. Introverted anger and emotional states	8, 9, 10, 13	26%
8. Foster Child fantasy	25	24%
9. Actual participation in social work	17 (b)	20%
10. Compensations indicated	gen'l	17%
11. Ideas of reference	19	14%
12. A-typical sex life	26, 27, 28	13%
13. Typical sex life (abstinence stated)	26, 27, 28	16%
14. Typical sex life (indulgence stated)	26, 27, 28	7%
15. Typical sex life (neither stated)	26, 27, 28	64%

VII

Summary and Conclusions

This paper has endeavored to present a working classification for the study of personality including the main divisions of Temperament, Self-expression or Strength, and Sociality. The traits selected stand, we believe, for fundamental forces in the human life, and form the needed basis of sociability, habit formation, and character. It may be said that personality means the definitely fixed and controlling tendencies of adjustment of the individual to his environment. They generally have a long and important history in the life of the individual. If we include in our definition the adjustment to non-societal objects, intelligence must also be comprised in our classification. Personality, in the stricter sense, however, may be said to be the adjustment tendencies of the individual to his *social* environment. It is essentially social in its bearings. Of the various traits, intelligence and temperament are probably for the most part inborn. The qualities of self-expression and sociality are probably in the main acquired by the reaction of the hereditary structure of the individual upon his social surroundings. In this field the persistence of childhood and adolescent influences are of vast importance, and the need of an understanding of personality formation by parents and teachers correspondingly imperative.

A well controlled process of rating individuals by associates is probably an adequate means of obtaining an objective notion of a group of personalities with which the results of tests devised for this sort of measurement may be correlated. The most promising suggestions for such tests and studies resulting from our investigation are as follows: a reaction study of miniature situations for ascendancy and other traits; a letter writing, ego-reference, and motor expression test for expansion; a test of judging facial expressions; the insight and self-evaluation index; an objectively and specifically stated questionnaire.

When the traits of personality are either rated or (better if possible) tested, they can be conveniently plotted in graphical form giving a picture of the individual. A refined impression is thereby gained by which we can know and deal with the person in an intelligent manner.

Certain types seemed to fall out from our fifty-five graphs; viz., the strong type of personality (extroverted) either social or a-social, and the weak type of personality (introverted) either social or a-social. We find interesting relations between these major types of personality and temperament itself (emotionality), e. g. the tendency of the extroverted individual to have narrow and strong emotions and of the introvert to have broad but superficial emotions. In general the emotionality of the strong type is of greater breadth and strength than the emotionality of the weak type.

The present classification and research is to be regarded as but the beginning of the investigation of personality. The development of a complete and sensitive instrument of individual measurement for personality as well as for intelligence is a distant but perhaps not an unattainable goal. Progress must be made along two lines: first, the theory and genetic study of personality and the isolation of recognizable traits which are truly fundamental, and second, the practical technique of refining impressions in the rating of individuals and of devising crucial tests of the various traits.

SELECTED REFERENCES

Personality Tests and Scales:

Bureau of Salesmanship Research, Carnegie Institute of Technology. Schenley Park, Pittsburg.
Test Number 9, Will-Temperament Test, Salesmanship Series (Modification of Downey Test.)

Downey, June E., The Will-Profile, A Tentative Scale for Measurement of the Volitional Pattern.
University of Wyoming Bulletin. Vol. 16, No. 4b, November, 1919.

Fernald, G. G.: The Defective Delinquent Class: Differentiating Tests. Am. Journal of Insanity, Vol. 58, No. 4, Apr., 1912. 523-592.

Moore, H. T., A Method of Testing the Strength of Instincts. Am. Journal Psychology, Vol. 27, Apr., 1916, 227-233.

Morgan, Eleanor, and others. An Attempt to Test Moods or Temperaments of Cheerfulness and Depression by Direct Recall of Emotionally toned Experiences. Am. Journal of Psychology, July, 1919. 302-304.

Pressey, S. L. and L. W., "Cross-out" Tests, with Suggestions as to a Group Scale of the Emotions, Journal Applied Psychology, Vol. III, 1919, pp. 138-150.

Pressey, S. L. and Chambers, O. R., First Revision of a Group Scale Designed for investigating the Emotions, with Tentatative Norms. Journal Applied Psychology, vol. IV, 1. Mar., 1920, 97-104.

Questionnaires and Outlines of Systematic Observation of Personality:

Fernald, G. G.: Character as an Integral Mentality Function. Mental Hygiene, Vol. II, No. 3, July, 1918, 448-462.

Franz, S. I., Handbook of Mental Examination Methods, pp. 170-176.

Hoch and Amsden, A Guide to the Descriptive Study of Personality, Rev. of Neurology and Psychiatry, II, 1913, 577-587.

Partridge, G. E., Outline of Individual Study.

Watson, J. B. Psychology from the standpoint of a Behaviorist, Chs. VI, XI.

Wells, F. L., Mental Adjustments, Chap. VII.

Wells, F. L., The Systematic observation of the Personality —In its Relation to the Hygiene of Mind. Psychological Review, Vol. 21, 1914. 295-332. (A good classification).

Experimental Researches:

Downey, June E., Some Volitional Patterns Revealed by the Will Profile. Journal of Exper. Psychology. Vol. III, No. 4, Aug., 1920, 281-301.

Hollingworth, H. L. Vocational Psychology, Chs. II, VI, VII.

Langfeld, H. S., The Judgment of Emotions from Facial Expressions. Journal Abnormal Psychology, Vol. 13, 1918-19. 172-184.

Langfeld, H. S., Judgments of Facial Expression and Suggestion. Psychological Review, Vol. 25, 1918. 488-494.

General Articles:

Fernald, G. G., Character vs. Intelligence in Personality Studies. Journal Abnormal Psychology. Vol. 15, No. 1, Apr., 1920. 1-11.

Rosanoff, A. J. A Theory of Personality Based Mainly on Psychiatric Experience—Psychological Bulletin, 17, 1920. 281-299.

APPENDIX A

PERSONALITY RATING OF ....

THESE RATINGS WILL BE TREATED CONFIDENTIALLY

Read these directions carefully. Rate the person named above on a scale of from 1 to 50, according to the place you believe he would occupy in a group of 50 *average college students,* in each of the following ten classifications. The extremes (1 and 50) are described below. Under "rating" place the number (any number from 1 to 50 inclusive) which you think indicates the relative position of the individual in the group. There will be 10 such ratings in all. Be sure you understand what is meant by each of the descriptions. Read them carefully.

NO.	TRAIT	RATING
I.	1. Most pronounced tendency of group of 50 average college men to take the *active* role, and to dominate, lead, organize, etc., in dealing with his *fellows*. 25. Average, neither distinctly active nor passive. 50. Most pronounced tendency of group of 50 average college men to be *passive* in contact with his fellows, to be led rather than to be a leader.	
II.	1. Most *highly emotional* in the group. Reacts emotionally to objects and situations with the greatest frequency, and to the widest range of things. 25. Average. 50. *Least emotional*. Reacts in phlegmatic manner most frequently, and to widest range of things.	
IIII.	1. *Deepest and strongest emotions* of any in the group. 25. Average. 50. *Most superficial and weak emotions* of any in the group.	
IV.	1. Most pronounced tendency of group to *direct his thoughts and acts outward*, away from himself, to be objective minded, interested in the world about him, etc. 25. Average. 50. Most pronounced tendency to *direct his thoughts inward* toward himself, to be subjective, brooding, "shut in," etc.	
V.	1. Most pronounced ability of group to see his virtues, defects, and other traits *as others see them*. 25. Average. 50. Most pronounced *lack* of this ability.	
VI.	1. Greatest tendency of group to engage in *social work*, social problems, reform, etc. 25. Average. 50. *Least tendency* to engage in social interests.	
VII.	1. *Highest general intelligenc* in group. 25. Average. 50. *Lowest* general intelligence.	
VIII.	1. Most pronounced tendency in group to *"spread himself,"* air his opinions (*either* objectionably or unobjectionably), *expand* his personality into all he does, etc. 25. Average. 50. Most pronounced tendency to keep his ideas and feelings to himself, to be reserved in exhibiting his personality in thought or act.	
IX.	1. Most pronounced tendency in group to *over-estimate his abilities*. 25. Average. 50. Most pronounced tendency to *under-estimate* his abilities.	
X.	1. Most *unselfish* in group. 25. Average. 50. Most *selfish*.	

Rated by (Signature) ....

(Kindly place in envelope and *seal*. This information is confidential, and will not be disclosed to the person rated.)

APPENDIX B

QUESTIONNAIRE

1. Show as specifically as you can how certain persons and events in your life have determined your present interests, habits, and traits of character.
2. (a) What vocation or interest made the strongest appeal to you in childhood? (b) At the age of 16? (c) At the present?
3. What subjects do you like best in college?
5. (a) Did you ever design or plan a new object or write an original production? If so, what? (b) How did it succeed?
8. How many times have you been so angry at a person that you could not forgive him (or her)?
9. (a) How many times have you been angry in the past week? (b) For what causes?
10. Give instances of what you do in thought or imagination or otherwise when you cannot vent your anger by definite action toward its object.
11. Are your emotions stable or are you easily upset?
12. (a) Are you given to day dreaming? (b) What is the content of such day dreams and what is their effect on you?
13. (a) How many times have you been punished unjustly? (b) For what causes? (c) What did you do about it? (d) How long did it bother you?
14. What mannerisms do you have that you know of? (e. g. Putting objects in your mouth, shuffling your feet, automatic movements while thinking, talking to yourself, etc.).
17. (a) Are you interested in social conditions and social service work? (b) What have you done along that line?
18. (a) Have you any hobbies or special interests? (b) Name them.
19. (a) Do you ever feel that people are talking about you behind your back? (b) What do you imagine they say?
20. In a group do you consider yourself reserved or assertive?
21. (a) Are you or have you ever been bashful? (b) At what age?
22. (a) Are you easily embarrassed? (b) Under what circumstances? (c) How easily do you recover your composure?
24. (a) Have you ever written comments in the margins of library books or other books not belonging to you? (b) About how many times?
25. (a) Have you ever fancied that you were a foster child—that is, that your supposed parents are not your real parents? (b) At what age and over what period of time? (c) Did you ever really believe this?
26. (a) How did you gain your knowledge of sex? (b) At what age?
27. (a) Is there anything repulsive to you about the sex relation? (b) If so, why?
28. Are there any events in your sex life which have influenced your life history? Specific statements are desired if you are willing to make them.

THE STANDPOINT OF SOCIAL PSYCHOLOGY

BY R. H. GAULT

PROFESSOR OF PSYCHOLOGY IN NORTHWESTERN UNIVERSITY
EDITOR OF THE JOURNAL OF CRIMINAL LAW AND CRIMINOLOGY

THE phrase "social psychology" implies a description of psychic phenomena as they are found in groups of various degrees of organization. The mere fact that individuals are in juxtaposition to one another in the lowly or highly organized group is only of secondary interest, though it is of real concern inasmuch as it affords an opportunity for the development of socio-psychic phenomena. But the phrase does not imply a description of *all* psychic phenomena. The pain, for example, that is occasioned by the window falling upon a finger, those pleasant experience that arise on a chilly day when the sun shining upon us through the window pane induces us to draw closer to the window, and a host of others, more or less analogous to these, are outside the circle of those that directly appeal to the student of social psychology. Truly, however, they may appeal indirectly to such a student, in which case the strength of their appeal is in direct proportion to the immediacy of their connection with unquestioned social phenomena. While I sit in my study, for example, the rumble of a truck upon the brick pavement outside is borne upon my ear to my disturbance. This in itself is of no interest to the social psychologist. But it suggests to me the situation of my newly acquired neighbor to whom I recommended this as a quiet street. I imagine, or I conceive him as assuming an attitude of reproach toward me, and I flinch somewhat at the thought that I may have been somewhat less than explicit and frank in my relations to him when he was considering moving into my neighborhood. The audible rumbling of the truck is the first step in the historical development of a series of definitely socio-psychic phenomena. The neighbor I imaged as having moved into the block in response to my own recommendation, and I am flinching in response to his disappointment as I image it. The experience of the young man in his attic room while preparing to participate in a debate a week later is meat for the social psychologist. The would-be debater is shaping and reshaping his argument always with one purpose in mind: to present such stimuli as will induce a favorable reaction on the part of the judges; and he has the while more or less distinct imagery of his prospective audience in attitudes of approval or of disapproval of this argument and of that one when stated in one and another form. Once more the Boy of '61 and the Boy of 1917 are caught up into a certain elan—into a national spirit—when they march up and down upon the village green with their fellows in companies. Why? Because they know and imagine that tens of thousands of other boys like themselves from the Atlantic to the Pacific are doing the same thing, and that all are doing for the same reason that they are: viz. in response to the same set of orders from Washington. Were it not that knowing and imagining are in this case links in a chain building up an elan, these boys would be merely in juxtaposition upon the green, each one a jumping jack carrying a gun, and the social psychologist would pass them by. Their juxtaposition without the conscious processes I have mentioned could never develop the striking social phenomena that war time affords.

The activity of the artist and the reformer are illustrations of socio-psychic phenomena also. What they conceive to be the unexpressed or half-expressed voice of human need and aspiration is their guide in control of their behavior. In other words, they are reacting to an imagery of other people than themselves, and these people are conceived by the reformer as more or less inevitably reacting in definite ways to what he himself is saying and doing.

The behavior of the organizer of a large enterprise is another case in point. This is social behavior and its success will depend upon the completeness of the organizer's understanding, and his capacity for representing in his own consciousness the probable reaction of other folk to his own scheme in detail.

The foregoing, I think, is sufficiently suggestive of types of conscious socio-psychic phenomena.

But our phrase implies not only conscious phenomena, but unconscious mechanical backgrounds of the human personality as well: those backgrounds by reason of which individuals are sensitive to the presence, real and imagined, of other people; to conventions and customs; to what is "in the air"; to the spirit of the age; to public opinion; to prestige; to ideals as expressed in art in its various forms, etc. This means that at any rate some human instincts come into the ken of the social psychologist as well as other acquired predispositions or complexes. The students of instincts and the Freudians (or better, the cousins of the Freudians, who, I think, take a saner view of the unconscious) have gone a long way toward suggesting how important are these backgrounds in the process of developing and organizing human social relations.

I may say here that the student of social psychology seems to me to be interested secondarily even in the forces and forms of physical nature in as much as they, on their part, serve as stimuli upon the population, inducing appropriate reactions thereto, that are fairly uniform among the members of the group, and ultimately settle into uniform habits. By this reason, each one is better able than he otherwise would be to understand his neighbors and to react to them, and to develop a spirit of unity.

To this point, I imagine, there may be no serious difference of opinion. Difficulty arises, if at all, when we begin actually to examine the phenomena and to analyze them with a view to developing a science. The very first empirical datum that comes to the hand of the psychologist here is an awareness—a consciousness of stimuli and reactions among people. This awareness may be perception or imagination or thinking. The instinct, the predisposition, the unconscious complex are inferences among others that we arrive at in our efforts to understand reactions, and very helpful ones at that. Other inferences may be more questionable. For example, there is something about group life, about co-operation among individuals, that leads us to talk about a crowd mind, a group mind, or a social mind. The individual in a crowd or in a highly organized group does not behave as does the same individual in isolation. In highly organized groups there grows up a keen feeling of unity and of identity from day to day, and there is a conviction that progress has been made and will be made in the future by the whole group, and that it stands for a certain set of ideals and purposes. These are probably the phenomena above all that prompt some students to postulate the social mind—however it may be phrased. To do so perhaps satisfies a desire for completeness and system when the term is used in the sense in which we employ it as applied to an individual. No objection can be made to the term when it implies *only* the facts, theories, ideas, purposes, traditions, etc., that are held in common by the members of the group. On another hand it is described as a super-individual mind—one that is in addition to the minds of individuals but of the same stuff as they are, and that co-ordinates and unifies them. It is beyond the methods of science to arrive at such a mind.

Once more this social or group mind is described as a "super-individual mind" which "consists of the same stuff as the individual minds; its threads and parts lie within these minds; but the parts in the several individual minds reciprocally imply and complement one another and together make up the system which consists wholly of them; and therefore they can 'only be described in terms of mind.'" Neither, probably, is there any serious objection to this use of the term when it is interpreted as it appears to be meant—excepting as it implies an organization of the purposes of many individuals and so prompts the question where such an organization rests.

Why should we talk about the group or social mind at all? What is a mind of such description supposed to do for us? It is to furnish the groundwork for our sense of social unity among individuals of the same class, state or nation, the basis for the spirit and effort of cooperation and progress amongst them; and for the alleged fact that individuals are changed between isolation and association with others. But above all the strongest motive for developing such a conception is probably the felt need for a passage from the individual to the social. It seems to me that all the phenomena for which we seek an accounting or an explanation can be included under these heads, and that setting out, at any rate, as structuralists, we can be satisfied without recourse to the use of such a troublesome phrase as "social mind." To explain:

No group possesses a stronger sense of unity than the family—not merely because its members have lived together for years, but because while living together they have grown intimately acquainted with one another. Each member knows each other's temper, habits, outlook, capacities, ideals, background of experience, ambitions and all that. He knows the interpretation of each other's gesture and vocal inflection. He can be sure that his brother's feelings are like his own or different, and when he infers from certain signs that his brother's reaction to a given set of conditions is like his own an enlarged sense of unity with his brother ensues. The same course is running between each and every other member of the family. Ultimately the result of prolonged and intimate familiar association is a sense in any member's consciousness of the inevitableness of a certain reaction on the part of every other member to his own actual or projected behavior, and in every member is the matter of course feeling that the family, as a whole, stands for certain purposes and is bending its way toward realizing them. Each one in his mind's eye, so to speak, sees that reaction, even though not in detail; the more critical the juncture the more vivid the detail. The unity is felt and taken for granted quite as we, in altogether ordinary circumstances, foresee and take it for granted that we will breakfast and scan the morning paper before beginning a hard day's work on the morrow. Wherever one member may be, near or far away, he is in some terms or other imagines the reaction of other members of the family to his behavior at present or to his plans for prospective behavior. He knows whether their attitudes can be made to his own and if so by what means. He can direct himself to the end of winning their approval. It is precisely at critical moments as I have already intimated, when he is doubtful what course he should pursue, that this imagery and this sense of unity with a family are strongest in him. I believe all I have said is in entire accord with the experience of each of us. Rob him of this capacity to represent others of his group, as occurs in some pathological cases, and the sense of unity and the capacity and motive for cooperation go by the board.

In like manner one may speak of club and school and army life. Each one understands, interprets, and mentally represents each other. A is satisfied and courageous upon discovering that B and C and each of the others is of the same mind as he and reacting to him and to each other. But B and C and each of the others is doing fundamentally just as A is doing because all are responding to much the same situations, and have an approximately common background of experience. Hence there is unity and preparation and courage for co-operation. *We need think here only of several individual minds whose objects or fields of attention considerably overlap,* whose reaction therefore are analogous one to another and recognized or arising from personal contacts. It is unnecessary to use the ambiguous term "social mind" or "group mind" exception in the sense that all minds in the community happen to cherish approximately the same objects.

It seems to me that this way of putting the case offers, as I stated it above, the passage way from the individual to the social; a passage that lies wholly within the individual himself—so that there is no real dividing line between the individual and the social; a passage way that implies no organization excepting that within the individual himself. The development of a nation then is secured by all those means by which each citizen can be made to represent others. It is an enlarged case of the family.

When preparations for international war are on, and when the war is being fought we have an illustration in broad scope of what

I am trying to say. A national morale or sense of unity is developed by directing each citizen's attention to the same posters and catch phrases and ideals, and as a partial means to this end by getting hosts of them to doing the same thing. In season and out of season it is borne in upon him with emphasis through the press, platform and other means that every one of millions in the population is doing and thinking just as he is in response to the same stimuli and to one another. Each citizen feels and works, consequently, as if every other citizen were at his elbow and as if each one were responsive to each other.

These forms of consciousness that, according to the thesis, play their part as I have suggested, take the course of forms of consciousness in other connections; they lapse and unconscious mechanism is substituted for them. Just as we can hardly be said to have a conscious relation to our coats but nevertheless do the appropriate thing with them when we find them in the morning, so with these social relations; the *consciousness* of them lapses and we do the appropriate thing without at any rate *definite* consciousness that we are in a social relation of unity with others. Thus the unconscious comes into the ken of the social psychologist both in the form of instincts which precede conscious action and of acquired complexes which both precede it and arise from it. But conscious phenomena are the first empirical data in this connection.

"THE SUB-NORMAL MIND VERSUS THE ABNORMAL"[1]

BY HENRY H. GODDARD, PH.D.

DIRECTOR BUREAU OF JUVENILE RESEARCH.

IT WILL be recalled that Binet and Simon in their study of the relation of intelligence to the development of language, prepared 25 abstract questions arranged as nearly as possible in the order of difficulty. Their nineteenth question was "when two persons discuss a question before coming to an understanding about the words, what happens?" To this, some children of eleven years of age gave the following answers: "It will happen that they contradict themselves." "They will talk nonsense." "They will not talk about the same thing." "They will get angry." "They will end in a dispute." What an epitome of one phase of the history of psychology! What happens when people discuss consciousness, perception, and a score of other terms? Let the eleven year old children answer, "they contradict themselves," "They talk nonsense," "They will not talk about the same thing," "They get angry," "They end in a dispute."

The terms abnormal and subnormal have not yet been the cause of any such unpleasant result, but they may at any time occasion their share of trouble if we go on discussing the not-normal without using accurately these terms. Here are two words with a clear distinction, which can be of great usefulness in clarifying our discussions if we can agree upon what we wish to connote by each one.

Up to the present time there is little or no consistency in the usage of the terms. For some writers, everything that is not normal is abnormal; for others, it is subnormal; for still another class of writers the terms are used interchangably. For example, the feeble-minded are as often called abnormal as sub-normal and a person of low intelligence may be called sub-normal when the condition is due to disease and not to arrested development.

The situation is the natural result of our lack of knowledge of the various conditions that we wish to describe and our consequent inability to use an accurate terminology. It seems, however, that we now have a sufficient understanding of the processes involved to enable

[1]Read at Chicago meeting of American Psychological Association. Division of Clinical Psychology. December 29, 1920.

us to agree upon a usage of these terms that will be strictly scientific and consequently useful.

Almost the first use of the Binet-Simon Scale in this country was made by Dr. Huey in testing out the entire population of the Lincoln Institution for the Feeble-Minded and by the writer in testing the population of the Vineland Training School. Since none of these inmates was found to have an intelligence above 12 years, it was inferred that this was the upper limit of feeble-mindedness and the lower limit of normality. It was further inferred that all persons who were old enough to have a higher intelligence but who had the rating of 12 years or less were feeble-minded or sub-normal. Samplings were made in other institutions for the feeble-minded with the same result. On the basis of these results, the American Association for the Study of the Feeble-Minded at its annual meeting at Lincoln, Ill., in 1910, tentatively adopted a classification of the feeble-minded which has become universally accepted, namely, those with a mentality of 2 years or less were to be designated as idiots, those of from 3 to 7 inclusive imbeciles and from 8 to 12 morons.

The view that everybody who tested 12 years or less was feeble-minded prevailed until the results of the mental tests in the army reduced this to an absurdity. The army findings that 10 per cent. of the soldiers had a mentality of 10 years or less and another 15 per cent. a mentality of 11, and 20 per cent. a mentality of 12, giving as a result that 45 per cent. of the army had a mentality of 12 years or less, threw an entirely new light upon the problem of sub-normality and feeble-mindedness. It is obviously not true that 45 per cent. of the population is defective and not everybody who is even 10 years old mentally is feeble-minded.

We have evidently been guilty of bad logic. In the early history of mental tests several students finding that various groups of farmers, housemaids and even some legislators who were obviously *normal* in the popular acceptation of that term, tested under 12 years, drew the hasty conclusion that the tests were unreliable.

It is now clear that the only thing at fault was the concept of who is feeble-minded. Had these investigators pointed out to us that there were great groups of people of 10, 11, and 12 year mentality who could not possibly be called feeble-minded they would have made a distinct contribution.

To replace ourselves on the right track we must call to mind the definition of feeble-mindedness. This has always included not only the mental level but the inability to get along in the world, "manage their own affairs with ordinary prudence and compete with their normal fellows." The error lies in the wrong inference that all who test 12 years or less are incapable of maintaining themselves.

The next problem can now be considered: Why are some 10 year olds feeble-minded and others not? If we accept provisionally the 13 year mind as the lower limit of normality, then we have the condition that some people with mentality of from 8 to 12 are sub-normal but not feeble-minded. This, as a matter of fact, we know to be true. We know that many people of low mentality are cases of mental disease rather than mental arrest. They are the psychopaths.

But although our knowledge is as yet incomplete, it is not probable that all who are not feeble-minded are psychopaths. In other words, it seems more probable that many people who are sub-normal according to the above definition are neither abnormal nor feeble-minded. What then, is the distinction between sub-normal and feeble-minded in these cases? According to definition of feeble-minedness the difference is in their ability to take care of themselves. In other words, a person of mentality from 8 to 12 is generally able to manage his affairs and compete in the struggle for existence unless in addition to his low mentality he is handicapped by other disadvantageous traits, such as, for example, high temper. A certain man of 10 year mentality could earn enough money to support himself if it was not for his violent temper whereby he continually loses his jobs.

One writer has suggested that in view of these new discoveries we must re-define moron. This is not necessary unless we wish to make the term stand for *all persons* with mentality 8 to 12. According to the classification adopted by the American Association for the Study of Feeble-Minded the term moron was to include that group of the *feeble-minded* who have a mentality from 8 to 12, not all persons from 8 to 12. The term moron is improperly used when it is applied to any person who is not feeble-minded, no matter what his mentality.

The term sub-normal would therefore seem to be applicable to the feeble-minded and to such other persons as have a mentality below whatever age may be agreed upon as the lower limit of normality.

It has been customary to speak of the various grades of intelligence as being ranged along an upward trending curve. On such a line, all below a certain established point could probably be designated sub-normal. They comprise the group that has not developed to the required level. This is in line with the long established custom of describing the feeble-minded as cases of arrested mental development. The organism is normal and functions normally as far as it goes but its development has stopped too soon.

By etymology the abnormal person is the one that deviates from the normal line. To include all such deviates our upward curved line as a diagram of developing intelligence must be extended laterally to become a band or ribbon which can be divided lengthwise by a line separating the normal from the abnormal. Precisely where that dividing line is to be drawn is not yet possible to say.. So far as adults of normal level are concerned this is the old question of who is insane and who is not.

The new contribution to this problem is the discovery that children and persons of low mental level are as often abnormal as sub-normal. In other words, our band or ribbon is divided lengthwise into the normal and abnormal and horizontally into the normal and sub-normal. The lower part of our ribbon is sub-normal and a section of that is both sub-normal and abnormal. It is important to note that abnormality in this sub-normal level may be the result, of the deterioration of a mind originally normal as well as of disease in a naturally sub-normal mind. It is perhaps of some use to think of this division on the basis of structure and function as it seems to be largely such a matter. The sub-normal person is one of incomplete structure; the abnormal is one of imperfect function.

If this view is accepted we should refer to the person, whose mind is found to be *functioning* badly, as abnormal. He might be either below, at or above the normal level. He would still be abnormal.

The key to the entire situation has been the discovery of the psychopathic child. As long as we thought that all persons below a certain mental level were cases of arrested development there was no necessity for distinguishing between sub-normal and abnormal. As long as abnormality in adults was not appreciated until they were definitely crazy, there was no need of the word abnormal other than as a synonym for insane. But with the advent of mental tests and substitution of accurate measurements for mere superficial observation and guesswork, we began to accumulate data, analysis of which showed the very beginnings of deviations in mental functioning. So that today we can see the possibility of diagnosing abnormal functioning of the mind with a nicety that compares to the old methods of psychiatrists as the Wassermann reaction compares to the old methods of detecting syphilis or the tuberculin test with the former slow and late detection of tuberculosis.

The discovery that many sub-normal children are psychopathic and not cases of arrested development explains many conditions that were formerly difficult to understand. For example, in our Vineland study of the heredity of the feeble-minded there were cases in whose families we found no other feeble-minded, no matter how far back we would go. We did find much nervousness and insanity and various other conditions indicating a neuropathic condition and following Tredgold we put this down as feeble-mindedness due to neuropathic ancestors; but this was never satisfactory. It is not good biology, and one was at a loss to know how insanity in the ancestors resulted in arrested development in the child. It is now clear (and this has been confirmed by going over the particular cases involved) that these children in the Vineland Training School, considered feeble-minded because of their low level of intelligence, were actually cases of psychopathy rather than arrest of development. Every observer and student of the feeble-minded in institutions has always been troubled by peculiar exceptions to what was believed to be the general rule in regard to the feeble-minded. Such for example, as the fact that the feeble-minded are generally, when well treated, quiet, well behaved, easily disciplined and agreeable persons on their own plane. But then we always had to provide for the exceptions. Some of these children were sly and persistently mean, subject to periodic outbreaks of temper or "spells." Some were liars, thieves, runaways or sex pervents. It is now known that these exceptional cases were either not feeble-minded at all but entirely psychopathic or that they had psychopathy grafted on to their condition of arrested development. In other words, they belong to our group that is both abnormal and sub-normal, in which case their subnormality is due either to arrested development or to deterioration from a higher level.

For years students of childhood have been puzzled by cases of persistent misdemeanor, those troublesome children whose conduct could not be accounted for. These children were often brought for examination, parent or teacher expecting that they would be found to be feeble-minded and thus their conduct would be explained. But to our surprise and annoyance many of these cases tested fully up to age and occasionally tested even above age. In such cases our only report could be "we do not understand why they behave as they do since they are of normal mentality." We were inclined to explain their conduct as due to environment, early training or the lack of it, or to any peculiar condition discovered. We now know definitely that as a rule these cases while not sub-normal were abnormal. They were cases of psychopathy or child insanity.

Again those who have worked with mental tests have repeatedly been perplexed by the fact that the child mind did not seem to follow the path marked out for it according to our best understanding. For example, here is a child that tests up to age, a year later he still ought to test up to age if he is making normal progress, but the actual tests a year later show that he has gained only 6 months or possibly has not gained at all. In other cases a child is a year or two backward at present and upon examination a month later he seems to have gained six months or a year or even two years. We tested the Vineland public school children on three successive years and expected to find all those who were not feeble-minded, that is who had not tested 3 or more years backward on the first occasion would have made their normal year's progress between each two examinations. While this was true for the great majority, there was a considerable percentage that was very disturbing to our theories because of their irregularities in this respect. Moreover, some of those who were considered feeble-minded on the first test, at least were 3 years backward, were found to have improved, possibly two years on the one year. All this is now perfectly understandable on the reasonable assumption that these cases were abnormal rather than subnormal or normal. In other words, they were psychopathic children.

It is not necessary at this time to point out all of the ways in which this concept of the psychopathic child straightens out our problems. It is necessary to note the consequences for future scientific work in the study of children. In the first place it must be noted that while this explains many anomalies in our previous work it also makes much of that work either of little or no value, or at least necessitates that it be scrutinized with great care. We evidently have been dealing with mixed groups either of sub-normals and abnormals (and have treated them as though they were all subnormal) or if studying normals, our groups have contained some abnormals. In other words we have included in our groups of feeble-minded many children who were not feeble-minded but psychopathic.

The intelligence Quotient is already going out of use, having proved to have much less value than we had hoped for it, even for normals, while with the psychopaths it has of course, no use whatever. It is possible to say when a machine is 75 per cent. completed but it is impossible to say when it is 75 per cent. worn out. In my judgment the term is mischievous at best because it leads us to think that we have something valuable when we have not. Still more serious is the fact that it may mislead us into accepting as satisfactory or even highly gratifying a condition that is positively dangerous. There are strong indications that most of the I. Q.'s of 150 are abnormals and require expert care and treatment rather than complacent pride in their accomplishments. What we want to know in all these cases of the not-normal individuals is not only the quantity but the quality of their minds.

Even mental level itself has a different meaning with the psychopaths than with the normal or sub-normal. Our concept of mental level is that a person has the intelligence of a child of a specified age and we recognize at once that this is only a convenient way of approximating his condition or getting a handy and more or less accurate picture of him. As a matter of fact a 30 year old man with a mentality of 10 is quite different in many ways from a 10 year old child of 10 year mentality. But when it comes to diseased conditions of the brain with the consequent disturbance of mental function the measurement of level is still less satisfactory. With the normal person mental level means that his mind has developed to about the point indicated and stopped which is a valuable piece of information. In the psychopath however, we have the condition that some of the mental processes are functioning normally and others have been more or less destroyed. Our tests give us the value of these different processes and then we *average* them and call that the mental level. For example, it is not uncommon to have a psychopathic child miss some questions in age 4 and pass some in age 14. We combine these according to the rules in scoring and say he has a mentality of 10. But it is obvious that this does not give even an approximate picture of his mind. The misleading character of such a procedure has already been mentioned when we spoke of those children who were so abnormal in conduct and behavior that it was thought they might be defective, but when examined they tested at age and we diagnosed them as normal individuals. The fact is they were far from normal but their deviation from normal was in function and a mere scoring up of tests of intelligence, gives, not deviations in function, but merely the structural level. The greater the degree of abnormality the less the value of expressions of mental level until with the violently insane mental level is practically meaningless.

The conclusion from all of this is obvious. The quantitative study of mind, the determination of mental levels, important and valuable and necessary as it has been, was only a preliminary step, a first stage; and having practically mastered that preliminary we must now proceed to the much more valuable work of qualitative analysis.

The devising of new tests and scales of intelligence will doubtless continue to be a useful exercise for undergraduate students, but from now on the real business of the clinical psychologist will be the qualititative study of mental functionings, the determination of the degree of abnormality and the significance of the abnormality as found in different mental processes.

It has long been suggested that certain forms of genius are akin to insanity. If this be true, it must mean that abnormal functioning in some processes makes for efficiency and usefulness, whereas in other processes it is destructive.

Summary

There is a structural development of the human being which may be called normal. There is a point below which, development is so incomplete as to make it extremely doubtful whether the individual can function as a satisfactory member of society. A mind of this low level may be called *sub-normal.*

When such a sub-normal mind is further handicapped by unfortunate temperament or disposition the individual is *totally* incapable of functioning as a member of society and is therefore feeble-minded.

At all stages of this structural development there is a wide range of *functioning,* there is a normal functioning, and there is a point beyond which the functioning may be said to be *abnormal* because such functioning renders the individual so different from the mass of human beings as to make him incapable of filling a useful place in society.

It is possible than in a few exceptional cases a functioning that must be termed abnormal may nevertheless render the individual unusually useful—genius?

Many former studies are worthless and the literature must always be carefully scrutinized before we can accept and apply the conclusions that may have been drawn from data that were assumed to be homogeneous but were not.

In future, cases should be carefully examined for functional peculiarities before one can be sure that one is working with a homogeneous group.

A GROUP SCALE FOR INVESTIGATING THE EMOTIONS

BY S. L. PRESSEY

STUDIES FROM THE PSYCHOLOGICAL LABORATORY
OF INDIANA UNIVERSITY

I. *The Pressing Need for Investigation of Other than Intellectual Traits*

THE extraordinary activity of the past three or four years, in the development and use of tests of general intelligence, has yielded a wealth of information with regard to the relation of intelligence to social and economic efficiency. And it is beginning to appear that intellectual traits may be distinctly less important than has been supposed, in conditioning delinquency, economic capacity, or even scholastic training. Thus, Doll[1] has recently shown that the inmates of a penitentiary may average in intelligence quite up to the average of the general population. Rosenow[2] has pointed out a common statistical error which has frequently led to the over-evaluation of the intellectual factor in connection with the interpretation of correlation coefficients, in the study of delinquency. Wells[3] has presented findings which indicate lack of any close relationship between intelligence and mental stability. A number of workers[4] have made clear the comparatively low correlation which is to be expected between college grades and score on the army intelligence scale. The writer has recently submitted data which suggest that character traits such as persistence and interest may be quite as important as ability, in conditioning work in grammar school.[5]

---

[1]Doll, E. A. The Comparative Intelligence of Prisoners. *Journal of Criminal Law and Criminology*. Vol. II, 1920, pp. 191-197.

[2]Curt Rosanow, "Is Lack of Intelligence the Chief Cause of Delinquency?" *Psychological Review*, XXVII (1920) 147-57.

[3]Wells, F. L. Intelligence and Psychosis. *American Journal of Insanity*, Vol. LXXVII, pp. 245—July, 1920.

[4]See, for instance, Anderson, John E.: Intelligence Tests of Yale Freshmen," *School and Society*, 1920, 11, pp. 417-20. The correlation between test scores and the first semester grades was found to be .37. Perhaps the largest body of such material has recently been reported by Bridges from Ohio University, at the Chicago meetings of the American Psychological Association, in December, 1920. The average correlation between grades and the army Alpha score, for a total of over five thousand cases, was found to be .35.

[5]Pressey, S. L. An Attempt to Measure the Comparative Importance of General Intelligence and Certain Character Traits in Contributing to Success in School. *The Elementary School Journal*, Vol. XXI, pp. 220-229.

Such studies emphasize the need for methods of investigating, in a highly systematic manner, individual differences in interests and emotional make-up. The present paper will (a) present an examination or "test" intended for such research, and will (b) emphasize two unusual features of this examination which the writer believes are of some general importance in connection with such work.

II. *The Tests*

The form to be presented was developed from two earlier attempts in this direction[6] and was put into final shape during the summer of 1920. The tests appear, each on one page of a small four-page folder, each page being 6 inches by 9 inches.*

The first page begins as follows:

X-O TESTS

DIRECTIONS: On each page of this folder there is a test. Work these tests in order, finishing each test before you go on to the next. Do not hurry, but work as rapidly as you can; your score will depend partly upon the quickness with which you work. Begin with Test I below.

TEST I t........... d............

Read over the twenty-five lists of words on the page below and cross out every word whose meaning is unpleasant to you—every word which you do not like. You may cross out as many or as few words as you wish; but be sure to cross out everything that is unpleasant.

1. disgust fear sex suspicion aunt
2. roar divorce dislike sidewalk wiggle
3. naked snicker wonder spit fight
4. failure home rotting snake hug
5. prize gutter thunder breast insult

....

25. boat yellow crazy indecent shame

[6]Pressey, S. L. and L. W. "Cross Out" Tests, with Suggestions as to a Group Scale of the Emotions," *Journal of Applied Psychology*, Vol. III, pages 138-150, June, 1919; and Pressey, S. L. and Chambers, O. R. "First Revision of a Group Scale Designed for Investigating the Emotions, with Tentative Norms," *Journal of Applied Psychology*, Vol. IV, pages 97-102, March, 1920.

*The blanks are being sold by C. H. Stoelting Co. 3037-3047 Carroll Avenue, Chicago.

FURTHER DIRECTIONS: Read through the lists again. Do not change any of the marks you have already made. In addition to these, draw a line around the ONE word in each list that is most unpleasant to you. If you are not sure, guess. If there is no unpleasant word in a list, find the least pleasant. Work rapidly; but be sure that you have a line around one, AND ONLY ONE, word in EVERY list.

When you have finished this test, turn over the page to Test II.

As has been indicated, the test consists of twenty-five such lines. In the first scoring of the test, the total number of words crossed out is first counted, and the number written in the space for the total—the line marked "t" at the beginning of the test. The number of times some other word has been circled beside the word most commonly chosen as most unpleasant, is then counted, and this number is written in the "deviation space," headed "d." Thus in the first line the norms show that the word chosen as most unpleasant by the greatest number of people is "disgust." If the individual in question circles any other word in this line, it counts as one deviation.[7]

The second test consists of twenty-five lines such as:

1.	BLOSSOM	flame	flower	paralyzed	red	sew
2.	LAMP	poor	headache	match	dogs	light
3.	BATH	naked	choke	tree	alone	danger
4.	KING	father	baseball	queen	rights	razor
5.	SLEEP	grade	ache	fright	tongue	worry

[7]The selection of words for this test was made in the first place on the basis of extended experience in work with the insane and with delinquents. The present form is the result of two revisions, involving a very careful study of the percents crossing out and circling each word. Each line has been planned to contain words of roughly the same amount of unpleasantness. The words are also arranged in a set scheme for purposes of analysis. The words are grouped as unpleasant because of their relation to emotions of disgust, fear, sex-feeling, and suspicion; finally there is a set of "jokers." The "jokers" are words known, on the basis of the preliminary results, to be pleasant or at least not unpleasant. There is one joker in each line. The jokers are aimed to give a check (particularly in the use of the tests with psychotic or feeble-minded cases) as to whether the directions were understood. That is, if the directions were thoroughly understood, none of these pleasant words should be marked.

The joker in the first line is "aunt," in the next line, "sidewalk," in the next line, "wonder," in the fourth line, "home," and in the fifth line, "prize." That is, the joker drops back one word in order, in each successive line; the joker is the fifth word in the first line, the fourth word in the second line, and so on, the series beginning over again—the joker being the fifth word once more—in the sixth line. This scheme makes it easy to follow the jokers through, in scoring. However, it is not a scheme easily hit upon by a person taking the test, or followed by chance, as an automatism, by a pathological case. Other groups of words proceed after the same fashion, the key being given by the first line. So the sex words run—sex, divorce, naked, hug, breast; the fear words—fear, roar, fight, snake, thunder, and so on. For a more detailed description of the plan and development of the test, the reader is referred to the second article mentioned in Note 6 above.

The subjects are told first to go through the test and cross out all the words in small letters which are connected or associated, in their minds, with the word in capitals at the beginning of each list. They are then told to go through the lists again, and draw a circle around the one word in each line which is *most* closely connected with the capitalized word. The first score is again in total of words crossed out (or richness in emotional association). The second score consists in total number of deviates from modal choice, in choice of words circled.[8]

The third test consists of twenty-five lines of which the five below will serve as examples:

1. begging swearing smoking flirting spitting
2. fear hate anger jealousy suspicion
3. dullness weakness ignorance innocence meekness
4. careless fussy reckless silly childish
5. poor extravagant sporty shrewd bad-mannered

The subjects are told first to cross out everything they consider wrong. Then they are told to go through the lists again, and draw a circle around the one thing in each list which they consider worst. Scoring is again in terms of total words crossed out, and total number of deviations in selection of the worst thing.[9]

The fourth test consists of twenty-five lists such as:

1. injustice noise self-consciousness discouragement germs
2. clothes conscience heart-failure poison sleep
3. sickness enemies money blushing failure
4. falling queerness religion dizziness boss
5. sin operation conspiracy lightning marriage

[8]As will be seen from close inspection, the words are chosen very carefully with reference to pathological conditions and criminology. This is, of course, an attempt to present a free association test in group test form; and it may be added that the words were taken in the first place from the Kent-Rosanoff Study (Kent, Grace Helen and Rosanoff, A. J., A Study of Association in Insanity, *American Journal of Insanity*, Vol. 67, Nos. 1 and 2, 1910).

[9]The test is, obviously, an attempt to put in a convenient group test form an ethical discrimination test. As such it has a long history. (See, for instance, Fernald, Guy. "The Defective Delinquent Class: Differentiating Tests," *American Journal of Insanity*, Vol. 68, No. 4, April, 1921). In general, an effort has been made to obtain judgments as to the comparative importance of different types of wrong-doing (as in the first list given above), or to obtain an indication as to the tendency of one's prejudices (as in the fourth).

The subjects are told, first of all, to cross out all the things in this list about which they have ever worried. Then they are to go over the lists a second time, and draw a circle about the one thing in each list about which they have worried most. Again the scoring is in terms of the total number crossed out (or anxiety tendency), and peculiar choices in words circled (or emotional idiosyncrasy). And again the test has back of it experience with abnormal personalities, and is obviously framed with reference to the investigation of certain anxiety states. The attempt was also made to involve the content of certain types of delusion, in mental disease.[10]

So much for the separate tests: in the first summarizing of the examination, the total number of words crossed out on all four tests is first summed, and is considered an indication of total affectivity or emotionality. The deviations are then added together, and the total used as an expression of "total idiosyncrasy."

Two special features of the examination, which the writer feels to be of very great general importance, remain to be pointed out.

III. *The Examination as an Exercise in Test "Form"*

In the first place, the examination carries further than any other test so far produced the possibilities of the modern group test in (a) condensation of material and problem, and (b) saving of time and labor.

(a) The examination is an extreme example of condensation of matter on the blank. Each word in each test is in reality a separate question,[11] in choosing words to be crossed out. This means a total of

---

[10]The words are, in fact, classified from this point of view, according to a scheme which runs: five, three, one, four, two. So the "hypochondriacal" words run as follows: germs, heart-failure, sickness, dizziness, operation. The melancholic and self-accusatory words run: discouragement, conscience, failure, religion, sin. The paranoid or suspicion words begin: injustice, poison, enemies, boss, conspiracy. The words chosen with reference to the self-conscious or shut-in personality begin: self-consciousness, clothes, blushing, queerness, marriage. The "neurotic" list starts: noise, sleep, money, falling, lightning. . . . As in the first test, the classification is not to be taken too seriously, but is at least suggestive, makes an interesting point of departure in analysis.

[11]For instance, the material of the last test is quite largely from Woodworth's questionnaire, used in studying neurotic individuals in the army. This questionnaire consisted of such questions as: Have you worried about smoking? Yes. No. The person taking the examination was to underline yes or no, according as one answer or the other were correct. Putting the questions in this way, it required an 11" by 17" sheet to ask 116 such questions. That same question is asked as unmistakably by including smoking in the lists of the writer's last test, the instructions being that all things about which the subject has worried are to be crossed out. But the form used in the writer's examination permits one hundred twenty-five such words, plus the twenty-five questions as to which thing in each list is most worried about, in a space 9" by 6". That is, a total of one hundred fifty questions is presented in this space.

125 questions to each test, or 500 in all. The second part of each test (selection of one word in each line to be circled) adds twenty-five items to each test, thus obtaining a double yield of score from all the materials. And the grand total thus becomes—600 items of score, all presented on the two sides of a 9 inch by 12 inch sheet!

Further (b) since each question is answered merely by a single stroke of the pencil in crossing through or circling, and since (an important consideration) there is very little reading in proportion to the number of questions asked, the average college student answers all these 600 questions in twenty-five minutes; the average adult takes little longer. Further, there is no technique whatever required in the administering of the tests. The tests are "self-giving";[12] all that is the examiner does is pass out the blanks, and collect them again as each subject finishes—there is no timing of each test to the second, no technique in giving or other special procedure. Finally, scoring is altogether objective, free from elaborate schemes of weighting, does not involve repeated rehandling of the first crude scores, or elaborate calculations; most important of all, scoring methods are altogether the same for all four tests. The blanks can thus be scored by untrained clerical help. And such works can obtain the first score on the entire 600 items in about three minutes; scoring on "differential units" (to be described shortly) requires less time. A 600 item examination can thus (1) be given by an examiner without any special training or preparation whatever, can (2) be taken by the average adult in about thirty minutes, can (3) be scored by any clerk in three minutes.

IV. Research Tests and "Differential Units"

The examination thus (the first special feature mentioned in the introductory section) embodies certain new ideas regarding test form which have permitted great condensation and reduction of material, and great conveniences and saving of time and effort in the using. It is only because of these mechanical advances that the second feature above mentioned is possible. The nature of this second special feature can perhaps best be indicated by saying that the examination is not, really, a single examination, but several examinations combined.

[12]The subjects are simply told, as the blanks are passed out, to "read the directions, and do what they tell you to do"; as appeared in the copy of the first test reproduced above, the directions for each test are printed on the blank. Since the tests are not time limit tests, the subjects simply finish one test and then go on to the next without any special directions; and since the directions are very thoroughly systematized, and similar, from test to test, there is little difficulty with the directions.

The usual method, in building a test, is to select the items for the test according to their value in measuring the particular element which the deviser wishes to investigate, and then (the selection of items determined once for all) to deal henceforth in terms only of total score. But the writer wished to use the examination for exploratory research in a number of fields. And he did not wish to base his selection of items for any problem of differentiation merely on a bit of preliminary work; he wished to be able to re-select and recombine his items as the work progressed, in studying any particular problem. So it was finally decided to combine in the examination a variety of materials (as in the last test, where items of possible significance with reference to five different types of mental abnormality have been combined), and to develop "differential units" for study of special problems. The result is that *total scores on the entire examination are the blurred result of a number of factors, and are of relatively little importance.*[13] However, *it is possible, from the mass of data yielded by the examination, to combine certain items in such a way as obtain, from the single examination, highly differential information with reference to a number of problems.* The point is of fundamental importance for the understanding of the examination. And to illustrate methods of developing and using such "differential units" the following bit of research is presented.

[13]The totals are, however, of some interest in a first appraisal of data. The following data from 114 college students (58 women and 56 men) are, therefore, presented, to give a general idea of the nature of these totals:

Words crossed out—25 percentiles, medians, and 75 percentiles in order: totals 200, 230, 260; test I 27, 41, 52; test II 41, 55, 70; test III 60, 73, 86; test IV 33, 46, 55. The average number of words crossed out in the five groups of test I run as follows:

disgust	fear	sex	suspicion	jokers
14.2	8.6	13.0	10.1	.3

Only one case crossed out as many as three jokers. For the five groups of test IV the following averages were found:

paranoid	neurotic	shut-in	depressed	hypochondriacal
9.3	9.6	9.7	11.1	9.8

Words circled:—25 percentiles, medians, and 75 percentiles in order: totals 41.6, 47.2, 51.7; test I 9, 11, 13; test II 8, 10, 12; test III 10, 13, 16; test IV 13, 15, 17. Modal choices run as follows: Test I—disgust, divorce, spit, rotting, insult, street-walker, cruel, dirty, sewer, drunk, stink, filthy, suck, illegitimate, vomit, cheat, slash, kill, sin, assault, abortion, pus, pox, disgrace, indecent; Test II—flower, light, naked, queen, worry, dark, strong, high, brave, truth, beautiful, baby, girl, chills, worms, figure, unfair, horrors, suspect, disappointment, trick, work, children, country, water; test III—swearing, hate, ignorance, careless, bad-mannered, snob, prostitute, lynching, smutty, thoughtless, divorce, illegitimate, stupid, immodest, indecent, chewing, stingy, street-walker, dope fiend, strike, broker, quitter, gossip, nagging, brutal; test IV—self-consciousness, clothes, money, religion, sin, accidents, insult, God, blues, unfairness, depression, loneliness, temper, business, syphilis, disease, forgetfulness, worry, fault-finding, medicine, tuberculosis, nervousness, habit, teacher, awkwardness.

The question was as to whether the examination might not be used to distinguish those college students who, because of lack of interest or other extra-intellectual reason, were doing unsatisfactory work (the third problem mentioned in the first section). The tests were given to 105 regularly enrolled college students, 29 of whom a few weeks later, at "mid-terms," received warning from the Deans' offices that their work in at least one class was unsatisfactory. The question is as to whether these 29 might have been distinguished from the remaining 77 in advance, by means of the tests.

The method was very simple and straightforward. The percent. of those warned and of those not warned, crossing out each word was first found. The ten words were then located in each test, crossed out by the greatest proportional per cent. of those who did not receive warnings, and the ten words chosen especially by those receiving warnings. A differential score for each case was then worked out by subtracting number of words crossed out, of the ten favored by those warned, from number crossed out, of the ten favored by those not warned. The combined differential result on test I, III, and IV made up the total differential score.[14] The results were then tabulated as follows:

	.... score on differential words													
	-7-8	-5-6	-3-4	-1-2	0-1	2-3	3-5	6-7	8-9	10-11	12-13	14-15	16-17	total
........warned	1	2	5	5	6	5	2	2	1					29
not warned.....					3	3	14	16	13	15	8	3	2	77

The first line of scores is, of course, the distribution for the cases warned. It will be seen that thirteen of those receiving warnings made differential scores overlapping not at all upon the scores of those whose work was satisfactory; over 80 per cent. of those below the twenty-five percentile were warned, in the total distribution.

In contrast to these results may be put findings with another large class, using the army scale alpha, as follows:

.... score on Scale Alpha ....

[14]The second test was found of relatively little value for this study,

The writer wishes to express his obligations to Miss Edith Hopkins for her careful work in making the routine tabulations throughout. The first tabulations of words crossed out (it might be added, for the benefit of any who may wish to undertake a similar analysis) were made onto unused blanks, and the conversions to a percent basis made with a slide rule. The total labor involved in such an analysis is not, then, great.

60	70	80	90	100	110	120	130	140	150	160	170	180	190		total
1		1	2		3	4	4	6	3	1	1	2		warned	28
1	1	2		6	9	10	12	13	11	6	9	2	1	not w'n'd	83

There is complete overlapping of the two groups; only 25 per cent. of the cases warned are in the lowest quartile.[15] It is further interesting to note that correlation of score on the differential unit of the emotional tests with average mark for the previous June, for a total of 46 cases for whom these marks were available, gave a coefficient of .58—as compared with the coefficients of .37 and .35 for the army scale mentioned in note 4.

V. Discussion

The above findings are obviously of the most tentative character, and in need both of further analysis and further verification. But they are at least suggestive. They suggest, the writer believes, two conclusions. (1) Investigation of emotional and characterological factors, by means of that carefully systematized and controlled method which is called "testing," is possible, and promises results of great value. (2) Recent developments in "test form" (and in statistical method) make possible the gathering of data of practically any type with a precision, a readiness, and economy of time and labor, undreamed of a few years ago. Careful study of these methods will well repay any investigator, in criminology, social work, psychiatry, or any related science.

VI. Summary

1. The paper presents an examination for investigating the emotions.

2. A very careful development of test form has made possible the inclusion in the examination of a total of 600 questions. Nevertheless, the entire set of tests is presented on two sides of a 9 inches by 12 inches sheet. The average adult requires less than thirty minutes to cover the entire 600 items. A blank can be scored in less than three minutes. The examination is self-giving.

[15] It should be acknowledged at once that the comparison is by no means so satisfactory as it should be, particularly as the differential unit was tried back on the group from which it was derived. But—the emotional scale is more differential than Alpha in crude total of number of words crossed out! For 38 per cent. of the students warned are in the lowest quartile in total number of words crossed out! Further data largely verifying these findings will be presented later.

3. Some data are presented to suggest that such examinations will be more accurate than the army scale Alpha in prognosicating unsatisfactory work in college.

4. It is urged that work along these lines is the pressing need, and that such an examination as just described, permitting research along a number of related lines, is likely to open up the field for investigation more readily than a test organized for only one specific purpose.[16]

[16]Since finishing the above paper the writer has received a very interesting letter from Miss Caroline Dreyfus of the United States Health Service Hospital, No. 58, New Orleans, in which she describes use of the "X-O Tests" as a basis for more extended individual questioning. For instance, on the last test, one individual circled the two unusual words "rivals" and "enemies" as matters most worried about. Questioning "led to the display of distinct ideas of reference which had not been elicited before in any previous examination. Another patient crossed out the word 'whispering.' Conversation about this led to confession of hallucinations which had been denied up to this time." Such results are, the writer feels, of no little interest.

It should also be added that the blanks for the test are now being handled by C. H. Stoelting Co., 3037-3047 Carroll Avenue, Chicago, Illinois; or they may be obtained from the writer.

REVIEWS.

The Psychology of Social Reconstruction. G. T. W. Patrick, Ph.D., Professor of Philosophy, University of Iowa. Boston. Houghton Mifflin Company. Pp. 260. Price $2.00.

THE AUTHOR'S purpose is the examination of some of the current and popular plans for social reform and the application of certain of the elementary principles of psychological science to these problems. He emphasizes repeatedly the need for a scientific, historical and psychological background in discovering a new social order which shall be based on human needs and human nature rather than on commercial or economic motives.

Man, who has hitherto been more or less of a puppet in the hands of such forces as evolution, revolution, climate, and industry, is now for the first time consciously and purposively attempting to direct his own fortunes. This is a hopeful sign. It is characteristic of our times that our sensitiveness to the evils of our imperfect social order should have increased, and that we should tackle them with a will to cure them. The exalted, self-complacent social mood of the early part of the twentieth century is undergoing a reaction; the veener slipping off which merely covered suppressions that were not properly sublimated or redirected; for society, as well as individuals, may have its "complex."

The inquiry into the psychological foundations of the new social order insists on a reorganization which will provide directly for the exercise of man's inherent and instinctive proclivities. He should be given a field for the expression of instincts like that of pugnacity, which cannot be suppressed, but which could and should be sublimated. Since the human unit changes slowly and society rapidly, the question before the social reformers should be, not the modification of human behavior to a new system, but the adaptation of a social order to the men who are to live therein. We must lay more emphasis on the material and equipment with which we have to deal. If our aim is an attempt at eliminating undesirable traits in human behavior, then education, rather than political and social institutions and new laws, should be the means. Human nature repressed will balk, and social discord will ensue. We may "abolish" private property but we cannot stifle the instinct of ownership. It is not the enjoyment of luxury and peace, but the pursuit of them, the struggle, that gives zest to life. Our social schemes are too visionary, too shadowy. They do not provide outlet for expression, either by substitution or sublimation, of the instincts inherited through thousands of generations. All we have offered to us is a standardized world, made safe and sure for ultimate stagnation. Our new plans should confirm to those laid down by nature. Dr. Patrick then treats of some of the more powerful instincts which demand satisfaction, and sees in such instincts as loyalty, devotion, sex and parental bent, group solidarity, and self-sacrifice, the springs of action from which the best in us may be drawn out. Yet in the proposed new order which gives no opportunity of expression for these fundamental needs of the restless, aggressive, aspiring man, it is assumed that art, literature, religion, patriotism, morality, will spring from wealth and leisure, which would be obviously impossible in a non-striving society.

Again, if one of the schemes proposed for his betterment were made effective, man who is not essentially a laborer, although he may have the instincts of creative workmanship strong in him, is placed in work that is mere toil. The problem is how to increase and distribute our goods, and at the same time adapt our industrial system to the mental make-up of its workers. Drudgery, in some way, will have to be vitalized by loyalty, emulation or love. We must be able to humanize, not socialize, our industrial society. The picture of injustice today is based on fictitious values, material comforts. There appears to be no attempt to break away from the pursuit of the dollar, no objections to the prevalent business ideals. The one common point of agreement is the matter of wage adjustment, the distribution of the fruits of labor. We find no opportunity allowed for each to earn for himself some gain or glory. This program of equal distribution of wealth would be ultimately followed by staleness, mediocrity, and degeneration. Communism may work for bees and ants but not for the achievingly inclined twentieth century man. Collective ownership, except in very narrowly integrated groups is a contradiction of terms. Addition to leisure may not be a safe experiment. It is in our work, not in our leisure, that we should find life. The arguments for internationalism are founded on commercial and industrial rather than social and moral grounds. In nationalism, the larger the group becomes, the more difficult the integration. Industrial partnership offers a possible but still uncertain solution.

In this centrifugal age of ours, of which self-expression is the keynote, we must be on guard to preserve the integration and solidarity which is essential for the existence of social discipline, which will maintain justice within the state, in the Platonic sense, and which will guarantee to the generations to come a like opportunity for social stability. Knowledge of the real sources of welfare, of values beyond comfort, leisure and material goods, will bring about happiness and self-realization and restore to society both religion and morality which were formerly the field for expression of the instincts of loyalty and submission. We must enlarge our conception of education, and no longer leave it to mere chance, to journalists, movies and other near-sighted but far-reaching media. Our northern type of people demands not merely idealistic schemes of revitalized religion, moralized education, rational eugenic principles and a just economic system, but insists that the program should be workable, should be established on a concrete basis. The confidence and respect of the people, formerly given to political and to social leaders, must now be transferred to science whose representatives must be experts. Science, hitherto all powerful in destructive devices should be turned to channels of construction, not merely to bring about remedial and repressive measures which temporarily may be productive of brilliant results, but to build up a vigorous manhood, strong to resist evils, insuring for posterity a racial health and stability whose energies shall flow to moral, aesthetic and social ideals.

While one catches the inspiration and enthusiasm of the author one can not help but wish that he had been able to give us some definite concrete scheme, based on his psychological theories, which could be made effective in this sorry world of ours. Mere references and somewhat vague suggestions leave the reader to a certain extent unsatisfied by their incompleteness. The way has been paved for the production of another volume, at a later date, in which we shall perhaps be offered a clear-cut program. If such a book should be forthcoming, we might suggest that a specific table of contents, including a subdivision of topics and section titles, would render it more serviceable as a practical discussion of a vital subject. The present work, while somewhat rambling and repetitive, will serve as a vigorous and inspiring introduction to its author's *workable program* of social reconstruction.

GLADYS C. J. SCHWESINGER.

PSYCHOLOGY AND FOLK-LORE. R. R. Marett, Fellow and Tutor of Exeter College. Reader in Social Anthropology, Oxford University. New York, The Macmillan Company, 1920. Pp. IX+275. $2.75.

IN a series of essays and addresses on various ethnological subjects, *Psychology and Folk-lore* presents a variety of appeals to the psychologist for the employment of his methods in a new and fertile field. Dr. Marett initiates the appeal by urging a more inclusive training for the field worker in anthropology. Technical and sociological preparation necessary to identify and collect systematically should be supplemented by psychological training to insure a more sympathetic approach to those primitive human beings who are the real documents supporting and shaping the theories of the scientist. The ethnologist collects his curios, and therein reads the life of the tribe; the sociologist studies his primitive colony in order to fit their customs and institutions into his preconceived theories of society. Objectively, from what he sees, he proves his hypothesis of material culture resulting from genius *in situ,* or else resulting from culture contact, whichever his bent. But the final history must come through the savage, the chronicler of the tribe.

The mental processes of primitive man are incoherent, not occidentalized. To his words and actions civilized motives and significance must not be attributed. To understand his folk-lore, and his medicine man, the anthropologist must know the primitive way of thinking and of doing. Although the savage is not akin to the mentally defective, he is as unique a problem. In emotions he is perhaps less elusive than in mental processes; and it is here, by a sympathetic study of his emotions, that psychology may assist in an interpretation of folk-lore. Behind customs, proverbs, folksongs, and superstitions are solidified emotions varying little from those of other human beings. The mind may provide quirks of expression, erratic impedimenta, but the emotion expressed or impeded is fundamentally the same for all. Moreover, since only that is likely to survive which has had sufficient affective accompaniment, so we may expect to understand the nature of survivals more adequately by studying the emotions of the race from which they come. Here psychology and anthropology unite to produce a truer "history of vital tendencies."

The essays of which *Psychology and Folklore* is the first vary in the extent to which their content lends itself to psychological analysis. Any activity, whether war dance or religious incantation, pot making rites or magic infusion for aigue, which involves the personal element is more readily understood when attacked sympathetically. With some of the specific problems the advantages of projecting oneself as much as possible into the life of the people is obvious.

Folklore, for instance, is not merely a set of fossilized customs; it is a living force. To interpret the dance, the drama, the song accurately the anthropolgist must himself acquire the emotion by actual participation—the doing to become the knowing. He thus tempers the dispassionate attitude of the scientific tabulator, lives his way into knowledge instead of raking scraps from the surface. Marett suggests that already psychology has offered theories which interpret folklore not as remnants of obsolete institutions now meaningless, but as crude offshoots of an incoherent, unintegrated mind. Chance, faulty associations easily lodged in an impressionable mind lie at the base of much superstitution and magic.

Savage demagogy is a question of prime importance for a complete understanding of savage society. Sociology assigns to psychology all questions of the mechanism of leadership, of which savage leadership in the person of the medicine-man is a strangely complex phase. Has progress and invention been due to a few superior minds who discovered how to impress their genius on the sluggish, imitative mass of inferiors—or has it been a group progress, a gradual modification from day to day? If anyone in savage society falls in the category of genius, it is the medicine man—for either he is an unscrupulous demagogue with the success due a genius, or endowed with more common sense than his fellow tribesmen, he is sincerely applying it. Much effort has been spent to determine the sincerity of the medicine man administering his magic cures. He must know that before he produces from his mouth the stones which are to effect a cure, he has taken them into his mouth. But considering the incoherent association of savages, the absence of any logical assembling of experiences, their suggestibility, and auto-suggestibility, their nervous instability and epileptic tendencies, the medicine man may *not* know what he has done a few moments previous to his miracle. It is such tangles that the psychologist may comb.

Dr. Marett has offered much interesting material for psychological treatment, but does not himself attempt the analysis. Throughout he reiterates the desirability of psychology to complete the equipment of the anthropologist. In spite of the blanketing of the personality in customs which send their creepers into every crevice of daily life, the instincts of primitive human beings are not deeply buried. In penetrating the lives of these imitative folk a completer knowledge of people is necessary in order to balance a knowledge of things. "Folk-lore," say Marett, "means more than the mere compilation of curious oddiments. It is the study of the life of the folk—insight into mind and character."

A useful synopsis precedes each chapter.

Ada L. Gould.

The Form and Functions of the Central Nervous System, An Introduction to the Study of Nervous Diseases. By Frederick Tilney, M. D., Ph.D., Professor of Neurology, Columbia University; Attending Neurologist, the Presbyterian Hospital, and the New York Neurological Institute, Consulting Neurologist, Roosevelt Hospital, New York, and Henry Alsop Riley, A.M., M.D., Associate in Neurology, Columbia University, Associate Attending Neurologist, New York Neurological Institute; Attending Physician, Neurological Department, Vanderbilt-Clinic, New York. Foreword by George S. Huntington, ScD., M.D., Professor of Anatomy, Columbia University. New York: Paul B. Hoeber, 1921. Large octavo XXIV + 1020 Pages, 591 Figures containing 763 illustrations, of which 56 are colored. Price, $12.00 net.

THE College of Physicians and Surgeons in New York has seldom published a more momentous contribution to medical education than this work from its neurological department—and in the hundred and fourteen years of its existence its instructors have made many contributions to Medicine and to biological science in general. Certainly not since Barker's "The Nervous System and Its Constituent Neurones" (1899) has America made so valuable an addition to educational neurology.

Like many other things in human life the work needs to be perceived, "immediately" experienced, in order to be appreciated. The preface veraciously states that "in addition to much original work, many sources have been drawn upon for neurological facts and interpretations. Chief among these have been the great modern masters of neurology, Cajal and Dejerine. The more recent contributions of distinguished English neurologists, including such leaders as Gaskell, Elliot Smith, Hughlings Jackson, Head, Sherrington, Horsley, Holmes, Campbell, and Wilson have provided a wealth of material," while the "American School" of neurology is adequately represented, besides,—Herrick, Huber, Jelliffe, Dana, Starr, et al. per terras.

The book is dedicated to Doctor George Sumner Huntington, Professor of Anatomy at Columbia.

This work, like the authors' "Introduction to the Study of Nervous Disease," is "designed to fill the gap between morphology and the practical requirements of clinical medicine. It aims to visualize the living nervous system, to make accessible an appreciation of its vital relation to the functions which go to make up life, as well as the defects in these relations which result in disease." As Professor Huntington points out in his Foreword, it tends to obliterate the evil "divisions commonly existing between premedical, preclinical, and clinical studies," (a reform started in the University of Oregon with the appointment of the "Professor of Zoölogy and Director of Fundamental Education in Medical Science"). Numerous pictures of parts of the brain as found in a large variety of the brutes, so that direct comparison is possible, provide material by which the student of animal psychology might considerably profit. (Stegosaurus, however, the ten-ton dinosaur with a sixty-gram brain (the size of that of a three-weeks kitten) is not noted.)

An interesting educative feature of the book is the twenty-five or thirty symptom-groups (syndromes) of as many important neuropathological conditions, adaptations of the case-history method. They serve to directly fix in the reader's mind the relation between functioning structures and their respective diseases. "By this method," as the Preface notes, "the anatomy and the physiology of the central nervous system are no longer permitted to remain as independent branches of medical science, but are here incorporated as essential parts of the practical knowledge necessary to the proper diagnosis and treatment of disease." Nothing is more essential certainly than this synthesizing reform in the old, over-analytic anatomies and even text-books of neurology. The psychological reader however, (and medicine is being forced, against its will, to acquire a little interest in the human mind!) the psychological reader will regret that a few pages of fine print (if nothing more) had not been devoted to taking the synthesis further into the far more interesting and not less essential realm of the stream of mind. This might have proven to be an excellent investment among the psychologists. For them mostly the book as it is will be just a bit, or further, outside their common range. Even if the book were written for medical folk, as the authors would doubtless say, every psychologist and philosopher of mind needs it literally in his thinking business,—and ought somehow to be coaxed into transferring the gist of it into his "end brain." Why this basal inconsistency of limitation, then, in the systematic integration?

On the other hand, the constructive physiologist, psychologist, sociologist, and such, will find here, especially in the numerous discussions of function under the various parts of the nervous system, what perhaps is the most comprehensive and useful summary of present opinions anywhere available. There is a very full and detailed description of the cortex (pallium), the newer material of Brodmann, Campbell, etc., in systematic completeness. In these details of the stratigraphy of the cortex, if anywhere, when we have found the interpretative key for opening up its mysteries, will be found the physical "basis" of mind (as a psychomotor adaptation). The student of personality will find in this book of

Tilney & Riley a skeleton of integration which perhaps, we shall learn ere long to clothe with a consistent tissue somewhat such as the behaviorist and every "good" psychologist besides seeks elsewhere in vain. For example, here is the whole scientific sanction of the subconscious aspects of the mind; and here too are the data through which the student of things-in-general i. e., psychology, can readily comprehend how affects color and often determine our thoughts; and just why the cortex represents movements but never muscles, and so on—just what he most needs to know!

Here is a synopsis of the contents of the work divided into fifty chapters: The Central Nervous System, Its Importance and Significance; Embryological Development of the Central Nervous System; The Unit of Structure of the Nervous System, The Nerve-Cell or Neurone; The Integration of the Neurones to Form the Nervous System, The Neurone Theory; Exposure and Investigation of the Spinal Cord in Situ; The Spinal Cord, Its General Character and Anatomy, Its Coverings and Circulation, Histology of the Cord Segment, The Function of the Gray Matter in the Cord Segment, The Function of the White Matter in the Cord Segment, Its Principal Syndromes; Removal of the Brain and Investigation of the Brain Case; The Medulla Oblongata, Encephalization and a General View, Relations, Surface Appearance and Anatomy, Internal Structure and Histology, Functional Significance, Principal Syndromes; The Pons Varolii, Significance, Anatomy and Embryology, Internal Structure and Histology, Functions and Principal Syndromes; The Cerebellum, A General View of Its Evolutional Significance, Relations, Surface Appearance and Anatomy, Internal Structure, Histology and Embryology, Its Functional Significance, The Principal Cerebellar Syndrome and Its Variations; The Midbrain, General Significance, Anatomy and Embryology, Internal Structure and Histology, The Functions and Principal Syndromes; The Interbrain, The General Significance, Anatomy and Embryology, Internal Structure and Histology, The Functions and Principal Syndromes; The Endbrain, The Cerebral Hemispheres; Surface Anatomy, Development and Comparative Morphology, Cerebral Measurements and Cranio-Cerebral Topography, The Coverings of the Brain, The Cranio-Cerebral Circulation, The Cortex; The Medullary Substance, Functional Significance and Principal Syndromes of the Medullary Substance, The Internal Nuclei, Functional Significance and Principal Syndromes of the Corpus Striatum, Cerebral Localization, The Somatic Motor Area, The Somesthero-Sensory, Visual and Auditory Areas, The Limbic and Insula Areas, The Parietal Frontal and Prefrontal Areas, The Internal Structure of the Hemispheres and the Ventricular System.

There is a useful Glossary of five pages; there are important references for supplementary reading; and a forty-three page index.

The 763 illustrations are little short of splendid, and none short of this large number. A series of diagrams showing the various columns, etc., through the cord and the brain-stem, cannot fail to be of great teaching value to visualizing students, young or old. The histology and the embryology are "complete" to this year of grace.

Very likely the work has "faults," but certainly the present reviewer is not one to search too diligently for them amid such a teeming wealth of neurologic virtues and excellencies. And it is a fact that he has none worth mentioning in mind.

The work is indeed an honor to its authors, their University and their Country. GEORGE VAN NESS DEARBORN.

NEUROLOGICAL CLINICS. Exercises in the Diagnosis of Diseases of the Nervous System. Given at the Neurological Institute, New York, by the Staff of the First Division. Edited by Joseph Collins, M. D., New York: Paul B. Hoeber, 1918.

This publication consists of a series of cases presented by the staff of the First Division of the Neurological Institute at their bi-weekly conferences.

The reports are characterized by their brevity, with the inclusion of the essential and important diagnostic points and the avoidance of unnecessary, long case-histories. This makes the reading and assimilation of the cases easy —which is not the case with the ordinary reports of this sort, especially neurological and psychiatrical presentations. MEYER SOLOMON.

LOCOMOTOR ATAXIA (TABES DORSALIS). An introduction to the Study and Treatment of Nervous Diseases. For Students and Practitioners. By William J. M. A. Maloney, M. D., (Edin.) Fellow of the Royal Society of Edinburgh; Fellow of the New York Academy of Medicine; Fellow of the New York Neurological Society; Neurologist to the Central and Neurological Hospital; Formerly Professor of Neurology, Fordham University, New York. Illustrated. D. Appleton and Company, New York and London, 1918.

This work by Maloney handles locomotor ataxia in a way which is appealing, interesting and instructive. After considering the relation of syphilis to tabes, he takes up the results of the syphilitic lesions in respect to motion, sensation, attitude and movement, the cranial nerves, the sensory and motor vegetative symptoms, and finally chemical disturbances. The diagnosis, course and treatment of the disease are then given.

Maloney lays particular stress upon the mental state of the tabetic. He pays particular attention to tabes as a cause of fear, fatigue and depression. He compares tabetic psychoses to prison psychoses. He thinks much of the value of psychotherapy in the treatment of this disease, and goes over the treatment in a thorough manner from this standpoint, in addition to all the other modes of attack.

The entire presentation is marked by sincerity and clarity.

I have found this discussion of locomotor ataxia more interesting and impressive than any other that I have read up to date.

Everyone who deals with or is interested in locomotor ataxia should read this work. MEYER SOLOMON.

BOOKS RECEIVED.

Psychology of Everyday Life. By James Drever. London. Methuen & Co. Ltd. Pp. IX plus 164. 6/ net.

The Psychology of Industry. By James Drever. London. Methuen & Co. Ltd. Pp. IX plus 148. 5/ net.

The Bolshevism of Sex. By Fernand J. J. Merckx. The Higher Thought Publishing Co. of New York, 1921. Pp. 207.

Lehrbuck der Experimentellen Psychologie. von Joselh Froehs, S. J. Herder & Co., St. Louis, Mo. Pp. XVIII plus 704. $5.25.

Education and World Citizenship. By Maxwell Garnett. Cambridge University Press, London. Pp. X plus 515. $5.

Exceptional Children and Public School Policy. By Arnold Gesell, Ph.D., M.D., Yale University Press, New Haven, Ct. Pp. 66.

The Punton Sanitarium

A Private Home Sanitarium for Nervous People

G. WILSE ROBINSON, M. D.,
Superintendent

30th Street and the Paseo :: :: Kansas City, Mo.

PETTEY & WALLACE SANITARIUM

958 S. Fifth Street
MEMPHIS, TENN.

FOR THE TREATMENT OF

Drug Addiction, Alcoholism, Mental and Nervous Diseases

A quiet, home-like, private, high-class institution. Licensed. Strictly ethical. Complete equipment. Best accommodations.

Resident physician and trained nurses.

Drug patients treated by Dr. Pettey's original method under his personal supervision.

Detached building for mental patients.

Dr. Barnes Sanitarium

Stamford, Conn.

A Private Sanitarium for Mental and Nervous Diseases

Also Cases of General Invalidism Separate Department for Cases of Inebriety

The buildings are modern, situated in spacious and attractive grounds, commanding superb views of Long Island Sound and surrounding hill country. The accommodations, table, attendance, nursing and all appointments are first-class in every respect. The purpose of the Institution is to give proper medical care and the special attention needed in each individual case. 50 minutes from Grand Central station. *For terms and illustrated booklet, address*

Telephone 1867 **F. H. BARNES, M. D., Med. Supt.**

A Modern Health Resort situated among the hills of Northern New Jersey, one thousand feet above the sea, forty-six miles from New York. A modern, steam heated building, broad verandas, sun parlor, good air, pure water, excellent table, delightful walks and drives through beautiful mountain scenery.

All Forms of Hydro-Therapy and Massage

A quiet, homelike place for semi-invalids, convalescents, neurasthenics and those desiring change of environment. Every facility for treating cases of neuralgia, sciatica, lumbago and rheumatism. **No tubercular nor objectionable cases.** Let us send you our booklet. Telephone 21 Newfoundland. **D. B. Drake, M. D.,** Supt. and Res. Phy., **H. H. Cate, M. D., Asst., Geo. A. Day, Asst. Supt.**